Fire in My Bones

Fred M. Wood

BROADMAN PRESS
Nashville, Tennessee

Library of Congress catalog card number: 59–5864

Printed in the United States of America

Affectionately dedicated to
Lillie Belle Wood
whose devoted companionship
beauty of character
and Christlike unselfishness
have strengthened my ministry
and made this work possible

Preface

Why another book on the Prophets? Some are likely to conclude that the present work is but another addition to the already overwhelming number of studies in Hebrew prophecy that have appeared in recent years. Yet those who are familiar with recent literature will at once realize that although much of real value has been written on the Hebrew prophets as a whole, or as individuals, comparatively little has been done concerning Jeremiah.

The studies in Jeremiah that have been made are primarily of two sorts. Some are of a technical nature, intended for specialized scholars and understood only by them. This was brought into sharp focus when a well-educated layman asked a theologian to suggest some books he might read to help him understand the basic thoughts of the biblical writers. Upon the conclusion of his attempts to master the suggested volumes, the perplexed layman said to his advisor, "Whom are these men writing for? One another?" Books on Jeremiah, written by scholars for one another, will elevate their mutual understanding but will leave the common man untaught.

Other works on Jeremiah are written for the layman, but usually they are of a devotional nature. These often help one in his devotions but not in his knowledge of Jeremiah; they do not drill deep enough to reach the richest treasures of the book. Only a knowledge of the Hebrew language and of the basic critical problems in the book can bring to life the great prophet.

Dr. Fred Wood has produced a rare study. Starting from a thorough knowledge of the basic problems of the prophecies, he has come to sound conclusions. These have been arrived at through years of study and original thinking. In 1948 Dr. Wood wrote his doctoral thesis at the Southern Baptist Theological Seminary under the title "A Chronological Reconstruction of the Life and Prophecies of Jeremiah." This excellent work has formed the basis for his further studies and has undergirded them. However, Dr. Wood has written the present book for the busy pastor and the interested layman. He uses terms of a nontechnical nature to express observations derived from technical study. Many sermon and devotional ideas will be found in the book, but, most of all, the reader will come to understand Jeremiah himself. He will be inspired by the prophet's insight and encouraged by his faithfulness.

CLYDE T. FRANCISCO

LOUISVILLE, KENTUCKY
July 12, 1958

Acknowledgments

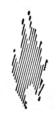

It was at Southern Baptist Theological Seminary that I first became interested in Jeremiah. I was beginning graduate work and Dr. Clyde Francisco, head of the Old Testament Department, asked me to consider making a thorough study of the prophet Jeremiah. It was through Dr. Francisco's encouragement and assistance that I completed my study. I wish to acknowledge my debt to this most dedicated professor. Dr. Francisco's scholarly interpretation and encouraging help have made a major contribution to this work.

I also wish to acknowledge my profound debt to my secretary, Mrs. A. E. Gibson, who has labored untiringly and most efficiently in helping me prepare my manuscript. She contributed willingly and devotedly to the arduous task, and I express my great appreciation for her work.

To other friends who have constantly encouraged me, I wish to say thank you for every word spoken and suggestion made.

FRED M. WOOD

MEMPHIS, TENNESSEE
October 14, 1958

Fire in My Bones

Contents

Introduction

Among the writings of Thomas Carlyle is found this striking statement, "Biography is the only true history." If this be true—and the more one reflects on it the more logical it seems—then the counterpart is nonetheless accurate, "A man can never be understood apart from the historical situation."

For that reason, if one is to understand the message of Jeremiah, he must approach it with an understanding of the day in which the prophet lived. He must have cognizance of every influence that came to bear upon the prophet's life. These opening pages are therefore an attempt to set the man Jeremiah in a historical framework that will show the relevance of his messages for the day in which he lived and lay the foundation for a larger application to our own day.

This book is not intended to be a biography of Jeremiah. It does, however, seek to trace the events of his life according to a chronological sequence. Far less do these pages profess to be a commentary, although at some points the author does attempt exegetical work. Neither is this volume intended to be a collection of sermons, although it is hoped it has some homiletical and expository value. The author would like to think that this is an interpretation of the life and message of

1

Jeremiah. An attempt has been made to present not only a chronological arrangement of the book but also a serious study of the progressive spiritual stages in the life of Judah's greatest prophet.

I

If one would understand Jeremiah, he must travel in imagination to the little village Anathoth, located just over the Mount of Olives some three and one-half or four miles northeast of Jerusalem. Strictly speaking, Anathoth, although included in the land of Judah, was located in the territory of Benjamin. According to the book of Joshua, it was one of thirteen cities set aside for the priests of Judah, Simeon, and Benjamin (Josh. 21:13–19; 1 Chron. 6:57–60). The small town was actually a suburb of Jerusalem, as it was easily within walking distance of the religious capital. Yet it was also a country town with all the characteristics which would belong to the remotest village exposed to the desert east of Jerusalem. The present town of Anata is generally conceded to be the site of ancient Anathoth, although some recent scholars are inclined to place the city of Jeremiah some half a mile distant, insisting that Anata is a city built after the destruction of the prophet's home. Whether this conjecture is to be accepted or not, one still may breathe the air of the village "situated upon the first of the rocky shelves by which the central range of Palestine declines through desert to the valley of the Jordan" and gaze with Jeremiah from his home and see the "land fall away in broken, barren hills to the north end of the Dead Sea."

They that wear soft raiment are in king's houses; those who shall be no mere reeds shaken with the wind but rather heavenly hammers to drive home truths for God must know discipline, and what better than the stern, sober, stabilizing discipline of the desert? In this same general vicinity and under similar environment grew Amos and John the Baptist. Indeed, during his temptations our Lord himself absorbed this atmosphere.

Anticipating by seven centuries the insult hurled at our Saviour's home, the people might have sneered, "Can anything good come out of Anathoth?" But it did, and across the same hills that Saul, the first king of Israel, walked as he sought his father's asses there ran a lighthearted lad who was to stand spiritually head and shoulders above his contemporaries.

II

When one seeks to train a boy to become a great man, he must begin with his grandfather, but the spiritual roots of Jeremiah go back three centuries beyond this limit. Jeremiah was "the son of Hilkiah, of the priests that were in Anathoth" (1:1). The history of the priestly family of Anathoth dates back to the time of David and Solomon. In the closing days of David's reign there arose two groups, each seeking to put one of David's sons on the throne. Joab sought to make Adonijah king and was aided by Abiathar the priest. They were opposed, however, by Nathan the prophet, Zadok, another of the priests, and of course, Bathsheba, all three of whom sought successfully to install Solomon as David's successor.

In true Oriental fashion there was a purge when Solomon ascended the throne. Adonijah and Joab were slain, but because he was a man of God, Abiathar was merely banished to the "country pastorate." Since that time the descendants of Abiathar, denied the privilege of ministering about the sacred things of the Temple, had nevertheless continued to perform the humble duty of ministering to the spiritual needs of the people of Anathoth.

There is still debate among scholars as to the relative purity of the worship at the "high places" of the local shrines. It is only fair to give proper motive to the reforming parties who sought to centralize worship at Jerusalem. Surely they were far more interested in correcting moral abuses than they were in gaining power. It seems imperative that we recognize there must have been perversions and immoralities in connection with the worship at the local shrines. In thinking of Jeremiah's home, however, we are strongly constrained to agree with George Birmingham: "It is possible, and indeed likely, that the religious life of Anathoth was purer than that of other local shrines, owing to its proximity to Jerusalem." This writer would add "probably due also to the continuing influence of Abiathar." Certainly the example of Abiathar added its weight.

III

According to many Old Testament scholars, Jeremiah was born about the middle of the seventh century before Christ. In this writer's opinion, the prophet was born closer to 640 than 650 B.C., but the ten years difference does not militate against this observation: Jeremiah's birth was halfway between the two great invasions of Judah by foreign powers. In 701 Sennacherib endeavored to follow up the victories of Tiglath-pileser, Shalmaneser, and Sargon in Syria and Israel and his own successes in Judah by demanding the complete capitulation of Jerusalem. After his defeat and retreat Judah enjoyed a period of peace from foreign invaders. With the exception of the disciplinary action of the King of Assyria against Manasseh (2 Chron. 33:11–13), it seems that no outside army invaded Judah for a full century.

Internally, however, a cancerous condition was developing. At the death of Hezekiah, Manasseh came to the throne, and for more than half a century (fifty-five years) he not only failed to follow the pious policies of his predecessor but as king of Judah he "seduced them to do that which is evil more than did the nations whom Jehovah destroyed before the children of Israel" (2 Kings 21:9).[1] In the midst of this spiritual darkness a godly couple named their boy "Jehovah hurls," hoping, no doubt, that he would be used to throw against Judah's downward plunge the full force of himself and God's message. Was there still hope, or had Judah sinned away her day of grace?

Two other factors should be noticed. First, although they were but a cloud the size of a man's hand, the Babylonians were rising. Their time had not yet come, but long before Habakkuk and Jehovah discussed Judah's moral dilemma, the great Judge of the earth was working a work. Although at the time of Jeremiah's birth Babylon's future was probably not yet visible even to the most discerning, by the time he began his ministry thoughtful students of world conditions realized that anemic Assyria would be replaced by fresh vigorous blood; and since it could never be "Rahab that sitteth still" (Isa. 30:7), it must of necessity be the Chaldeans who were striving for their place in the sun.

Second, regardless of those who disagree, the Scythians cannot be glibly eliminated from Old Testament history. The ancient historians may have let their imagination and their nationalism run wild under certain circumstances but, as Davidson insists, prophecy begins in cataclysmic events. What other historical event or people can serve as the background for Jeremiah's early messages of "hell fire and brim-stone" (4:5 to 6:30) and Zephaniah's "Day of the Lord," with its wrath, trouble, distress, wasteness, desolation, darkness, gloominess, clouds, trumpet, and alarm against the fortified cities? The early ministry of Jeremiah must be studied against the backdrop of the Scythians who, according to Herodotus, were carrying on raiding expeditions along the western coast of Palestine at that very time. It was a great day to be alive. Could anyone who was spiritually minded have refrained from being a burden-bearer for Jehovah?

IV

No man ever lived through a generation of more significant events. No preacher ever had the opportunity to hold aloft the banner of God in the midst of such strategic days. Five kings sat on the throne during the active ministry of Jeremiah. Two reigned only three months each, but the other three not only ruled a number of years but were also involved in international events.

Josiah (639–608 B.C.) was one of the best kings who ever sat on Judah's throne. In the eighth year of his reign he began to seek after the Lord; in the twelfth year he began to purge Judah and Jerusalem from the high places; and in the eighteenth year, during a cleansing of the Temple, a law book was discovered which became the basis for a great reformation. Scholars are divided as to Jeremiah's part in the reform movement, but the evidence indicates that Jeremiah at first joined hands with those who were enforcing the royal edict but later began to perceive the shallow nature of the whole program. In 608 Josiah rushed to halt the north-bound army of Pharaoh Necho. It seems that good king Josiah, because of the success of the reform movement, had become puffed up with a sense of his own importance and sought to push his good fortune too far. Whatever the motive that prompted such action, Josiah was killed at Megiddo, and one of the godliest kings in Judah's history went to his final resting place.

Jehoahaz, who reigned three months, was placed on the throne by "the people of the land." This, no doubt, means that he was the popular choice of Judah. It is interesting to note that he was not the oldest son of Josiah. Jehoiakim was two years his senior, but for some reason the people preferred the younger son, perhaps because of the older son's pro-Egyptian tendencies. Necho, however, deposed Jehoahaz, put a heavy tax on the land, and put a new king on the throne and the old king in chains.

Jehoiakim (608–597 B.C.) was the Egyptian name of Eliakim; he was, of course, not only a protégé but also a puppet of Egypt. Inasmuch as Necho had placed him on the throne, he was at first loyal to Egypt, but in the early years of Jehoiakim's reign Nebuchadnezzar came up against him, and Jehoiakim became his servant for three years. This was, in all probability, the invasion referred to in Daniel 1:1, when the "Lord gave Jehoiakim king of Judah into his hand, with part of the vessels of the house of God; and he carried them into the land of Shinar to the house of his god" (v. 2). It was during the reign of Jehoiakim that the battle of Carchemish was fought between Assyria and Babylon. This conflict in 605 settled the matter of international power and made Babylon undisputed leader in military and political strength.

The remaining years of Jehoiakim were days of royal apostasy and national degeneration. He was without character, conscience, or concern, and under his leadership all hope of Judah's spiritual restoration disappeared. Building

7

his palace with forced labor, following in the footsteps of Manasseh, who filled Jerusalem with innocent blood, and finally burning the book of the law, Jehoiakim has gone down in history as synonymous with infidelity, irreverence, immorality, and ignominy.

In 597 the crisis came. Jehoiakim's rebellion against Nebuchadnezzar reached its zenith, and the Babylonian army came to deal once for all with Judah's king. Although we are uncertain as to the particulars of his passing, Jehoiakim met his death during the reckless and riotous period which accompanied this second invasion. The darkest days of Jeremiah were during the reign of this wicked king.

Jehoiachin, the son of Jehoiakim, followed, but his rule was brief. Following the advice of his mother, and perhaps the prophet Jeremiah, he surrendered to Babylon. Although he was placed in prison, the historian tells us that thirty-seven years later the king of Babylon "did lift up the head of Jehoiachin king of Judah out of prison; and he spake kindly to him, and set his throne above the throne of the kings that were with him in Babylon, and changed his prison garments. And Jehoiachin did eat bread before him continually all the days of his life: and for his allowance, there was a continual allowance given him of the king, every day a portion, all the days of his life" (2 Kings 25:27–30).

The last king to sit on the throne of Judah was Zedekiah (597–586). The greatest shortcoming of Zedekiah was not wickedness, although he was an ungodly man, but indecisiveness. When Zedekiah rebelled against Babylon, Nebuchadnezzar's army surrounded the city. For eighteen months Jerusalem was besieged. At last the city fell. Zedekiah fled but was overtaken in the plains of Jericho. He was carried captive to Babylon. The political activity in Judah after the fall

8

of Jerusalem was the tragedy of a nation without a leader. The small remaining group went to Egypt, and Jeremiah accompanied them.

For a fuller discussion of these historical happenings the reader is referred to each of the chapters in the following pages. Jeremiah's ministry should never be considered isolated and detached from the events of his day. He spoke, as do all prophets, to the generation in which he lived.

V

As one approaches the book of Jeremiah, he faces an almost insuperable difficulty, namely, the lack of chronological arrangement. Harry Emerson Fosdick says,

As a lad I started to read the Scripture through according to the familiar schedule, three chapters each week-day and five on Sunday, by which we were assured that in a single year we could complete the reading of the Book. I got safely through Numbers and Leviticus, even Proverbs did not altogether quench my ardor, but I stuck in the middle of Jeremiah and never got out. I do not blame myself, for how can a boy read Jeremiah in its present form and understand it? [2]

This may well serve as a starting point, emphasizing as it does the difficulty of comprehending the book of Jeremiah as it is arranged in the English Bible. It is not only the boy who finds difficulty with the prophecies of Jeremiah. For all its readers the roll of Jeremiah is a hopeless jigsaw puzzle of prophetic discourses, biographical material, and historical narratives arranged without much, if any, plan of chronological sequence. The prophecies cover a period of more than forty years, but the order of time is repeatedly violated without apparent reason.

No clear principle seems to have determined its arrangement. As a result, one who attempts to read the book straight through finds himself in a state of constant bewilderment. The book, it is true, begins with an account of the prophet's call and earlier prophecies. But the successive chapters wander hither and thither over the long and rugged course of Jeremiah's active life. Without warning the scene shifts. The same chapter may contain sections which belong to widely different periods in the prophet's ministry. In other sections the reader may find himself with no clue to the situation or period of the prophet's life reflected in the portion he is reading. It is not strange that one scholar calls the book a "conglomeration of prophecies," and another designates it "the most unreadable book in the Bible."

As a concrete illustration of the chronological confusion, one needs only to look at some of the chapters which are definitely dated in the text. Chapters 21 and 24 are designated as occurring during the reign of Zedekiah. But chapter 25, though appearing later in the text, is dated "in the fourth year of Jehoiakim, . . . king of Judah." Chapters 27 and 28 belong to Zedekiah's reign, but chapters 35 and 36 go back to the time of Jehoiakim. The latter chapter goes as far back as the fourth year of that king.

Even more tantalizing is the fact that chapters 26–45, for the most part, contain biographical material. Pfeiffer calls this section the "Biography of Jeremiah." Normally it would be expected that if any kind of writing should be chronological, it would be biographical data. But the last chapter of the "Biography of Jeremiah" contains the description of an event which occurred at least twenty-one years earlier than those in the immediately preceding chapter. The Jewish captives carried to Babylon by Nebuchadnezzar were addressed in words of comfort several chapters before the announcement to Jehoiakim that the event was imminent. The prophecies relating to the foreign nations form the bulk of the latter portion of the book. Most of them, if not all, were delivered long before the final overthrow of Jerusalem and Judah.

The writer has attempted to arrange these prophecies in a chronological sequence. The result of his work is included at the close of the book.

VI

In his "Memories of Men Who Saved the Union," Don Piatt says, "Hero worship is healthy. It stimulates the young to deeds of heroism, stirs the old to unselfish efforts, and gives the masses models of mankind that tend to lift humanity above the commonplace meanness of ordinary life." Byron expressed the universal longing when he confessed,

> I want a hero: an uncommon want,
> When every year and month sends forth a new one.

Of course, the one cruel and cutting fact about heroes is that they are made of flesh and blood, and Homer reminds us, "Heroes as great have died, and yet shall fall."

Jeremiah had a hero—a prophet who had lived, as did Jeremiah, during the last generation before his nation's doom. The similarities between the messages of Hosea and Jeremiah are too striking to be merely coincidental. Hosea's influence on the prophet from Anathoth is apparent even to a casual reader of the two books. Not only did Jeremiah find in Hosea a teacher but, even more important, he also found a kindred spirit. Ancestrally, there were strong ties between them, for both were from Israel. S. L. Brown, agreeing with Holscher, contends that Hosea's home was in "that strip of country, mountainous yet fertile, between Bethel and Jerusalem and

11

looking over the Jordan valley which belonged to the tribe of Benjamin." If so, the prophets were from the same geographical background. It is not difficult to conceive a mental image of the lad's devouring eagerly the words of the prophet who had witnessed in Israel that which the young man progressively came to be convinced was in the not too distant future for Judah. For hours at the time he must have meditated upon Hosea's nation and his own. Partly by natural endowment and partly through the deep impression made upon him by his hero, Jeremiah developed an exceptionally tender and emotional temperament, sympathizing intensely with the people to whom he must deliver God's message, a message of the certainty of moral retribution upon a people who were speeding down the precipice to spiritual bankruptcy and national chaos.

Some scholars believe that Jeremiah's interpretation of God's will for him to remain unmarried was influenced largely by Hosea's unfortunate domestic life. Of course, according to the words of Jeremiah, the command was because the times were unsettled, and "they shall die grievous deaths: they shall not be lamented, neither shall they be buried; they shall be as dung upon the face of the ground; and they shall be consumed by the sword, and by famine; and their dead bodies shall be food for the birds of the heavens, and for the beasts of the earth" (16:4). There may, however, be some truth in this suggestion, for God often speaks through the experiences of others. There is no doubt that Jeremiah felt that his, like Hosea's a century before, would be the final voice to a nation's dying agony.

Jeremiah was indebted to Hosea, his hero, not only for his theological concepts but also for the form these thoughts took as the prophet delivered his messages. Both men used these images: the concept of the relation of Jehovah and Israel as that of husband and bride; the characterization of the worship of other gods as fornication and adultery; and the evaluation of Israel's sojourn in the wilderness as the ideal period in the life of the nation and the time in which the relationship between Israel and Jehovah was most nearly perfect.

The following list of parallels between Hosea and Jeremiah is suggestive but by no means exhaustive:

Jeremiah	Hosea
2:2 ff.; 3:8	1–3; 6:4; 13:5
2:8	4:4 ff.; 5:1; 6:9
2:18	7:11
2:31 ff.	1:2; 2:2 ff.
3:22	14:1, 4
4:3	10:12
5:30; 18:13; 23:14	6:10
7:9	4:2
7:22 f.	6:6
9:12	14:9
14:10	8:13; 9:9
30:9	3:5
30:22	2:23

VII

One final word is necessary in order that Jeremiah may be properly introduced. To understand the message we must understand the man. It was more than a series of sermons that God sent to Judah as a last desperate effort to halt her mad race to doom. It was a man. In our own day we often find that what the sermon cannot do the man will be able to accomplish. Sermons may be dull, but life is always vital.

The great fact of Jeremiah's personality was the fact of a loving heart. He, like the One whose life he foreshadowed, wept because of the sins of his people. Because he was only human he had his shortcomings. Perhaps his greatest fault was his impatience both with his people and his God. Love, however, covers a multitude of sins, and people will forgive an impatient minister if they are convinced he possesses an unselfish love for them. But it must be love, and it must be unselfish.

Jeremiah's greatest teachings came out of his heart. Early in his ministry he was alarmed because he felt certain that judgment was coming immediately. He spoke of being "pained at my very heart; my heart is disquieted in me" (4:19). When reform swept the land, he was carried away with its enthusiasm. Snapping back suddenly to reality at the death of Josiah, he saw the tragedy of a nation deceived by a shallow religious program and shouted, "Oh that I could comfort myself against sorrow! my heart is faint within me" (8:18). The bitter days of Jehoiakim's ungodly reign brought a rapid maturity to the prophet. It was then that he learned the true meaning of prayer. Discovering through his prayer life that the world's chief problem is a heart "deceitful above all things, and . . . exceedingly corrupt" (17:9), he came to possess in his own heart a fire shut up in his bones which made it impossible for him to hold back from delivering the divine message. By the time Zedekiah came to the throne Jeremiah was convinced there was a higher loyalty than to the government. To the captives in Babylon he urged submission to the foreign power, and with the group left in Judah he plead for surrender to the invading army. The prophet was convinced that Judah's hope lay not in seeking to defend a country guided by a corrupt leadership but in finding Jehovah by seeking him with her whole heart (29:13).

The destruction of Jerusalem and the burning of the Temple prepared the prophet to understand completely that which he had partially and progressively comprehended throughout his ministry: fellowship with God is the basis of all religion. Thus he could speak of the divine ideal as a community of people in whose hearts God's will was written (31:33). Underlying all of Jeremiah's thinking and teaching was his faith in the future. Even when Jerusalem was surrounded by the Babylonian army, he purchased a piece of property in nearby Anathoth, affirming with a confident heart, "Houses and fields and vineyards shall yet again be bought in this land" (32:15).

Many writers have endeavored to list the teachings of Jeremiah. This author would only point to Jesus and say that more than any other prophet Jeremiah anticipated the Master and his message. It is easy to understand why some scholars believe the contemporary fulfilment of the Suffering Servant in Isaiah 53 was found in Jeremiah's life and why at Caesarea Philippi the reply to Jesus' question was spontaneous: "Some say that thou art Jeremiah" (Matt. 16:14).

1
Fanning the Flame

All the prophets of Israel and Judah stand as inspiring personalities, but Jeremiah is the one who possesses the most universal appeal. Each student of the man sees in him some different trait of character. Gordon calls him "the rebel prophet"; Church labels him "Jeremiah the puritan"; and to John Paterson he is the "prophet of personal religion." Skinner looks upon him as a "moral analyst"; Chappel sees him as "the reluctant prophet"; while to many he is "the prophet of the decline and fall of the Southern Kingdom." Jeremiah's long and varied ministry, no doubt, accounts for the variation of descriptive titles.

But when he called Jeremiah, God commissioned him to a twofold task: "See, I have this day set thee over the nations and over the kingdoms, to pluck up and to break down and to destroy and to overthrow, to build and to plant" (1:10). Jeremiah's life, his preaching, and his suffering in his endeavor to warn the people of the approaching doom of Jerusalem emphasizes that this, more than any other, is an inclusive and comprehensive description of the ministry of the prophet.

Prophetic preaching must always, of course, contain these two major emphases. The writer of Ecclesiastes speaks of "a time to plant, and a time to pluck up that which is planted"

(3:2). This is a reversal of the commission to Jeremiah, but the basic principle is the same. It was Jeremiah's lot to pluck up ritual and plant religion, to pluck up the legal approach and plant the spiritual approach, to pluck up Temple worship and plant Jehovah worship, to pluck up the old covenant in the letter of the Law and plant the new covenant in the spirit of the coming Messiah.

Chapter 1 contains the call of Jeremiah to the office of a spokesman for God. It is always a great moment when God speaks to a man. It is an even greater moment when God speaks to a boy.

The Time (vv. 1–7)

The time in the history of the nation is important. This was Judah's last opportunity. Her light was flickering. During the days of Isaiah she had almost "gone under." But because Hezekiah had taken his troubles to the Lord's house and had spread them before Jehovah (Isa. 37:14), God had come down from Zion to fight for his people and like a bird hovering round about the city had protected Jerusalem (Isa. 31:4–5). The city had become once more "a quiet habitation, a tent that shall not be removed, the stakes whereof shall never be plucked up, neither shall any of the cords thereof be broken" (Isa. 33:20).

But that was another day—another generation—another century. Hezekiah's good reign had been followed by fifty-five years of the most wicked of all Judah's kings. For more than half a century Manasseh had sought to undo all the good that Hezekiah had made possible through his religious reforms. In fact, the writer of Kings declares that Manasseh had brought the land to a worse state than it was during the days of the Amorites before Joshua had led the Israelites into the Promised Land (2 Kings 21:11). One writer has described the reign of Manasseh in graphic words: "Politically, it was a whirlpool. Morally, it was a cess-pool." Could there be worse?

Amon succeeded Manasseh, and when he began to follow in the footsteps of his father, some of the servants, rather than tolerate another reign like that of Manasseh, conspired against the king and put him to death in his own house (2 Kings 21:23).

Josiah then became king in 639 B.C. at the age of eight. He fell under the influence of the prophetic party and from the beginning was a twig bent in the right direction. He made minor reforms in his youth. It was not, however, until the eighteenth year of his reign (621) that the great reformation began. Jeremiah was called in the thirteenth year of Josiah's reign. There is virtual agreement among scholars that this was the year 626—a great date in Judah's day and a great epoch in prophetic history.

We see also the time in the economy of God. Jehovah told Jeremiah that he was called from eternity. "Before I formed thee in the belly I knew thee, and before thou camest forth out of the womb I sanctified thee; I have appointed thee a prophet unto the nations" (1:5). We shall never, of course, understand fully how to reconcile the foreknowledge of God with the free will of man. Both are true, even though our minds cannot bridge the chasm. Skinner endeavors to give us an insight when he says, "The sense of predestination in Jeremiah's consciousness means the conviction that the endowments of his whole nature, his physical and moral environment, all the influences of heredity and education that had shaped his life and made him what he was, had worked together under the hand of God to prepare him for the task to which he is now summoned." [1] Wordsworth expresses the truth of this statement in his immortal lines:

> I made no vows, but vows
> Were then made for me; bond unknown to me
> Was given that I should be, else sinning greatly,
> A dedicated spirit.

We see again the time in the life of the prophet. Jeremiah says that he was a child. The Hebrew word *na-ar* is normally the word for a very young man. It is true that the same word is used to describe Joshua (Ex. 33:11) when he was forty-five years old. The subsequent ministry of Jeremiah emphasizes, however, that at the time when God spoke Jeremiah was an extremely young man, probably even a small child. Let no one minimize God's voice to a child. Robert Hall was converted at twelve years of age; Matthew Henry at eleven; Isaac Watts at nine; and Jonathan Edwards at seven.

The Touch (vv. 8–9)

Jeremiah was not as responsive to the divine call as Isaiah. Many writers have commented at length on the contrast. Suffice it to say that Jeremiah did not volunteer for service. He was drafted. All his life he remained an unwilling spokesman. He did not want to begin, and many times he wanted to quit. But Jeremiah had the marks of a true prophet: "If I say, I will not make mention of him, nor speak any more in his name, then there is in my heart . . . a burning fire shut up in my bones, and . . . I cannot contain" (Jer. 20:9).

The problem of Jeremiah was different from that of Isaiah. The Lord touched the mouths of each of these prophets but for a different purpose. Isaiah's mouth was touched for cleansing. He was a young man with a consciousness of un-

19

clean lips. Jeremiah's mouth was touched for empowering. He was a child with a consciousness of inadequate lips. It is interesting to note that Ezekiel and Daniel had similar experiences. The former was given a roll with the message of God for the people. He was told to "open thy mouth, and eat that which I give thee" (Ezek. 2:8). He did, and "it was in my mouth as honey for sweetness" (Ezek. 3:3). Daniel's experience was late in his ministry but was no less vivid and vital. In his vision of the son of man (Dan. 10) the prophet fell with his face to the ground when "one in the likeness of the sons of men touched my lips" (10:16). All four of the major prophets thus received God's touch. Isaiah was touched for cleansing, Jeremiah for empowering, Ezekiel for food, and Daniel for strength.

We need to remember constantly that it is the touch of the master's hand that makes a Stradivarius of the violin. One of the greatest preachers of yesteryear stammered until he was nearly through college. When God called him to preach, he was touched as was Jeremiah of old. The greatest eloquence a prophet can possess is the God-given eloquence of the divine touch.

The Task (v. 10)

It has already been observed that Jeremiah's task was twofold. All preaching is thus divided. The prophet was called upon "to pluck up and to break down and to destroy and to overthrow." He was also called "to build and to plant" (1:10). Regardless of how thorough the tearing down process, the preacher must have a positive program if his work is to be effective and enduring.

Let us, however, while emphasizing the necessity of the positive, remember that there must first be a "destruction of the devilish." Before the grain of wheat produces it must fall into the ground and die. Before the farmer plants he must plow up the roots. "Cease to do evil" must precede "learn to do well." Repentance for sin must precede faith in Christ. There is a great demand for the positive approach in thinking and preaching. This is good, but let us remember that the positive thinking of the Sermon on the Mount is preceded by the negatives of Sinai. The wrecking must always pluck up and break down in order to pave the way for the builders.

But the kingdom of God is never built on mere negations. Mature morality is always a higher concept. The world is hungry for affirmations. The motto of a firm in Texas, "We can wreck anything," is good for them. But God's people are not in the wrecking business.

The Tree (vv. 11–12)

One writer has a beautiful interpretation of these verses. It was January or February of the year 626 B.C. Jeremiah was in a rural section. As he walked down one of the paths in a meditative mood, he saw the bud of an almond tree, which was to the Jew one of the first signs of the coming of spring. God said, "Jeremiah, what do you see?" The lad replied, "A shaqed." Shoqed is a word meaning "that which is awake"; its root also produces the word for "an almond tree." God replied, "Thou hast well seen: for I watch over my word to perform it."

This was a message of great assurance for Jeremiah. He saw that God is active in the affairs of history. He is not some transcendent being unable or unwilling to intervene in the time of his people's need. He is awake (shaqed) and watching (shoqed) over Judah's destiny.

Kittel, the German scholar, says, "It certainly was not accidental the year 627–626, when he [Jeremiah] was called to prophesy, was the year in which the great King Ashurbanipal lay down to die, and that his death gave the signal for the opening of the final chapter of Assyrian history."[2] Babylon under Nabopolassor was entering the struggle for world dominion. Egypt was watching with hopeful eye the decadence of the Assyrian empire. Jeremiah was called to be a prophet to the nations.

Jehovah was telling Jeremiah that he would watch over the message. He would make certain that the word does not return void. It will be performed. God was ready to go into action. The long delayed and long deserved judgment was about to arrive. After a long period of spiritual freeze, Judah's springtime was approaching. God's activity was about to begin. It may be an activity of judgment or of mercy as the people will.

A story that comes out of the English Parliament illustrates this point. One member, a devout Christian, arose and suggested that the British foreign policy be based on the Sermon on the Mount. A skeptical sneer greeted him as one replied, "If we do this, God help England." The calm reply of the Christian was, "Have no fear; if we base our foreign policy on the Sermon on the Mount, God will help England." So God was watching his people and watching over his people as he prepared to go into action either for Judah's doom or Judah's deliverance.

The Terror (vv. 13–16)

These verses contain the second of Jeremiah's two visions. Jeremiah was passing by a cottage, and God directed his attention to a seething pot or a boiling caldron. This was a commonplace object near every cottage. Upon three sides there were stones, while the fourth was kept open. The fuel was placed here to feed the fire. Although scholars disagree on the technical meaning of the vision, the message is clear. Judgment was coming from the north. Jehovah was watching world affairs and would soon act. The verses immediately following verse 14 are much like those which God spoke to Jeremiah's contemporary, Habakkuk: "Behold ye among the nations, and look, and wonder marvellously; for I am working a work in your days, which ye will not believe though it be told you. For, lo, I raise up the Chaldeans, that bitter and hasty nation, that march through the breadth of the earth, to possess dwelling-places that are not theirs" (Hab. 1:5–6).

The Triumph (vv. 17–19)

These two visions were "strong meat" for a small child. It is not strange that he recoiled and insisted that he was inadequate for the task. But the closing words of the chapter assured Jeremiah of ultimate victory. "Be not dismayed at them, lest I dismay thee before them. For, behold, I have made thee this day a fortified city, and an iron pillar, and brazen walls, against the whole land. . . . And they shall fight against thee; but they shall not prevail against thee: for I am with thee, saith Jehovah, to deliver thee" (1:17–19).

Again the call of Isaiah comes to mind. Isaiah was cautioned against optimism, while Jeremiah was comforted against pessimism. Isaiah was told that he would fail. He succeeded, however, for the city of Jerusalem was saved. But Isaiah, according to tradition, died a martyr's death. Jeremiah was told that he would succeed. He failed, for Jerusalem fell. But Jeremiah in his last days was a hero, and he probably died a peaceful death.

Every prophet, regardless of his generation or his popularity, succeeds if he is faithful in declaring God's will. Every prophet who compromises his message fails, though he win world acclaim with the fickle multitude.

There is a great distinction between fame and popularity. William Hazlitt said, "Fame is not popularity. . . . It is the spirit of a man surviving himself in the minds and thoughts of other men." George Curtis said, "My advice to a young man seeking deathless fame would be to espouse an unpopular cause and devote his life to it." Oliver Wendell Holmes speaks of worldly fame as "the scentless sunflower with its gaudy crown of gold."

Jeremiah was to be a man of fame. But his fame was not to be his popularity. To Jeremiah was given the privilege of preaching. Many years later Paul said, "Woe is unto me, if I preach not the gospel" (I Cor. 9:16). Jeremiah's triumph was to be not his fame but his faithfulness.

2

Can a Bride Forget?

The section 2:1 to 4:4 forms a separate and distinct unit in the preaching of Jeremiah. It is a rather lengthy oracle concerning the religious failure of the nation Judah. Many Old Testament students believe this material represents the prophet's inaugural message—his first public sermon. There is a section, 3:6–18, that is a problem. The difficulty is that the train of thought from 2:1 to 3:5 is interrupted by 3:6–18 and is resumed in 3:19 and continued to 4:4. A thorough student of the book must see and deal with this fact.

There are two ways of dealing with the matter. One is to say that in compiling the book a mistake was made and this shorter address was placed in the middle of a larger address. The shorter message has a beginning, a body, and a conclusion. It deals with the relative faithfulness and faithlessness of Israel and Judah. The prophet declared that Judah should have profited and taken warning from Israel's folly and consequent punishment. It concludes with the promise of Jehovah that if Judah will return to him, the land shall be the center of a spiritual religion for the world.

The other approach is to maintain that the separate oracle is a parenthetical comparison of the two nations. Anyone who has preached or spoken in public to any extent recognizes immediately that this is possible and even probable.

It is not easy to find a closely knit train of logical thought in this passage. There are, however, several themes in the message. The central strain is that of Judah as an unfaithful bride. Around this major theme are gathered several other thoughts.

An Unequaled Heritage

Centuries before Jeremiah appeared on the scene, Moses concluded his series of oratorical pleadings with a searching interrogation, "Who is like unto thee, a people saved by Jehovah?" (Deut. 33:29). Hosea, several generations earlier, had spoken of his people's heritage in these words, "When Israel was a child, then I loved him. . . . I taught Ephraim to walk; I took them on my arms. . . . I drew them with cords of a man, with bands of love . . . I laid food before them" (11:1, 3–4). Isaiah had spoken of the nation as a vineyard from whom God had expected grapes but had received wild (the Hebrew says "stinking") grapes (5:1–7). But Jeremiah pictured the heritage of Judah as that of a bride.

There is no more appealing figure of speech for the relation between God and his people than that of a bride. This figure was adopted by Paul to express the intimate relationship between Christ and his church. Of course, there had been no literal wedding between Jehovah and Israel, just as there will be no wedding in the sky. These are symbols used to convey spiritual truths. Jesus said, "In the resurrection they neither marry, nor are given in marriage" (Matt. 22:30).

Jeremiah was saying for God, "No nation ever had such a beginning as yours. I remember your early devotion. Israel was a peculiar treasure of the Lord. She belonged to God exclusively. Remember the honeymoon days." These verses are reminiscent of the closing days of Joshua: "I gave you a land whereon thou hadst not labored, and cities which ye built not, and ye dwell therein; of vineyards and oliveyards which ye planted not do ye eat" (Josh. 24:13). Was Jeremiah adding his own personal touch to Joshua's words as he said, "And I brought you into a plentiful land, to eat the fruit thereof and the goodness thereof" (2:7)?

Looking down the corridor of the centuries, it is no far cry to our own nation and our own day. The very date of the discovery and settlement of America was in the providence of God. Columbus set sail in 1492, just as the effects of the free-thinking Waldenses and Anabaptists were being felt. By the time America was colonized Luther had nailed his theses on the door at Wittenberg, and the Reformers were rediscovering and reinterpreting the Bible. Moreover, our own nation was not settled by Spain and thus disciplined by the Inquisition. It was, rather, settled mainly by a Bible-loving and Bible-reading group of people. One writer says that Columbus was originally sailing on a course which would have landed him near the center of the Atlantic coast on the mainland of what is now the United States. A flock of birds flying southward caused him to turn; thus the Spanish flag was never the predominant flag on American soil.

Roger Babson and a friend were once talking about North America and South America. Said the friend, "Why is it, Mr. Babson, that South America has far more natural resources and potential wealth, and yet North America has developed in such a superior way?"

Mr. Babson replied, "I think this is the reason. The people who settled South America came in search of gold. The people who settled North America came in search of God."

Listen to Jeremiah's words: "I remember the devotion of your youth, your love as a bride."

An Unheard-of Sin

But something is now radically wrong with Judah. She has forgotten her honeymoon days. The orange blossoms have been killed by the spiritual freeze of Judah's national life. In this passage there is not so much a listing of specific acts of sin and transgression as there is a basic fact of disloyalty—Judah had departed from her God. This was the source of all her sins. Alexander Maclaren says, "Every act which is morally wrong is religiously a departure from God; it could not be done, unless heart and will had moved away from their allegiance to Him."

Jeremiah pictured this unheard-of sin in a graphic manner. Judah had done worse than any nation. One could go to the east (Kedar) or to the western extremity (Kittim) and he would never find a nation, even a heathen nation, leaving its gods. But look at Judah! There was a gushing fountain with food around it. All she must do was stoop and drink. Judah, however, preferred to ignore the feast which had been placed before her and dig her own cisterns which at their best would be "broken cisterns, that can hold no water" (2:13). There is a basic principle of life in this passage. When man leaves that which is right and godly, he must carry on compensating activity. Man's mind will not be idle. If he does not worship God, he will invent a god to worship.

Judah's sin was unheard-of in another way. The religious leaders had been equally guilty of spiritual infidelity. "The priests said not, Where is Jehovah? and they that handle the law knew me not: the rulers also transgressed against me, and the prophets prophesied by Baal, and walked after

28

things that do not profit" (2:8). Hosea, a century earlier, had seen a vital relationship between the religious leaders and the people. In our own day we see this truth again and again. Let a pastor remain at a church for a number of years and the church will unconsciously be a reproduction of his character. It is true that the institution is indeed the shadow of the man.

Again Judah failed to learn from God's chastisements. The Lord chasteneth his loved ones, and Jehovah had smitten the children, but in vain (2:30). Amos had warned Israel in a similar manner:

And I also have given you cleanness of teeth in all your cities, and want of bread in all your places; yet have ye not returned unto me, saith Jehovah. And I also have withholden the rain from you, when there were yet three months to the harvest; and I caused it to rain upon one city, and caused it not to rain upon another city: one piece was rained upon, and the piece whereupon it rained not withered. So two or three cities wandered unto one city to drink water, and were not satisfied: yet have ye not returned unto me, saith Jehovah. I have smitten you with blasting and mildew: the multitude of your gardens and your vineyards and your fig-trees and your olive-trees hath the palmerworm devoured: yet have ye not returned unto me, saith Jehovah. I have sent among you the pestilence after the manner of Egypt: your young men have I slain with the sword, and have carried away your horses; and I have made the stench of your camp to come up even into your nostrils: yet have ye not returned unto me, saith Jehovah. I have overthrown cities among you, as when God overthrew Sodom and Gomorrah, and ye were as a brand plucked out of the burning: yet have ye not returned unto me, saith Jehovah (4:6–11).

Isaiah had joined his contemporary, Amos, in urging his people to recognize God's chastising hand.

Why will ye be still stricken, that ye revolt more and more? the whole head is sick, and the whole heart faint. From the sole of the foot even unto the head there is no soundness in it; but wounds, and bruises, and fresh stripes: they have not been closed, neither bound up, neither mollified with oil. Your country is desolate; your cities are burned with fire; your land, strangers devour it in your presence, and it is desolate, as overthrown by strangers. And the daughter of Zion is left as a booth in a vineyard, as a lodge in a garden of cucumbers, as a besieged city (1:5–8).

God sent these judgments because he loved his people. Judah would not learn what the psalmist learned: "Before I was afflicted I went astray; but now I observe thy word. . . . It is good for me that I have been afflicted; that I may learn thy statutes" (Psalm 119:67, 71).

Moreover, Judah had failed to profit by her sister Israel's mistake. The parenthetical section, 3:6–18, deals with Israel's folly and Judah's failure to learn from Israel's judgment. Backsliding Israel had shown herself more righteous than treacherous Judah. This was perhaps not true in a literal sense, but Jeremiah's argument was that Judah should have returned to God because she had Israel's example to teach her that it is folly to walk in the stubbornness of an evil heart.

An Unbearable Condition

The sins of Judah had brought about an abominable situation in the land. The land had become polluted with idolatry and immorality. Few people of our day understand the relation of idolatry and immorality. The fallacy of idol worship is more than the fallacy of bowing down to sticks and stones. The folly of idol worship is that it has no ethical or moral compulsion because there is no personal God of character and holiness to serve as a constraining force to righteous living. Man becomes like that which he worships. Christians are to be holy because the God whom they worship is holy. The greatest sin of Judah's day was not the name by which she called her God but the perverted character which she developed because of the worship of "gods which are no god."

What was the result of such idol worship? Immorality had seized the land. Jeremiah frequently referred to the people's forsaking the Lord as spiritual adultery. "Surely as a wife treacherously departeth from her husband, so have ye dealt treacherously with me, O house of Israel, saith Jehovah" (3:20). "Judah . . . feared not; but she also went and played the harlot" (3:8). There is a twofold sense in which such passages are to be understood: first, the analogy of husband and wife with Judah's breaking the marriage vows; second, the worship of the idols which was bound up with sexual immorality. In fact, this worship was little more than the practice of licentious acts as a part of the religious ceremony. It is no wonder that Jeremiah shouted, "Be astonished, O ye heavens, at this, and be horribly afraid . . . saith Jehovah" (2:12).

An Unsatisfactory Remedy

Judah's sin was deeply engraved upon her character. This is, of course, the worst fact about sin. Acts lead to habits, and habits lead to character. The wickedness of the people had so imprinted itself upon the national character and upon individual lives that no mere reformation would solve the problem or absolve the sin. "For though thou wash thee with lye, and take thee much soap, yet thine iniquity is marked before me, saith the Lord Jehovah" (2:22). Sin is always against God. It is primarily a violation of the divine order. Sin against the moral order is a sin against the God of the moral order.

31

Sin against a fellow man is a sin against God's creature. Sin against the body is a sin against the temple of God and, therefore, against God. Mere reformation will not meet the need. When one has fallen into a cesspool of filth, it is not enough to say, "I will be careful henceforth where I walk." It was not enough for Judah to look unto the gods of her own hands for the cleansing which could come only from the God of character and holiness whom they had forgotten and whose standard of morality they had spurned and perverted. "As the thief is ashamed when he is found, so is the house of Israel ashamed . . . who say to a stock, Thou art my father; and to a stone, Thou hast brought me forth. . . . But where are thy gods that thou hast made thee? let them arise, if they can save thee" (2:26–28). "Truly in vain is salvation hoped for from the hills, and from the multitude of mountains: truly in the Lord our God is the salvation of Israel" (3:23, AV).

An Unforgettable Invitation

The only hope that Jeremiah held out for Judah was that she return to God. "Thou has played the harlot with many lovers; yet return again to me" (3:1). "Return, O backsliding children . . . ; for I am a husband unto you" (3:14). Hosea's conception of Judah as the bride of Jehovah, no doubt, colored the thinking of Jeremiah. As the eighth-century prophet had forgiven and restored Gomer, so Jehovah would forgive his unfaithful bride. A century before, Isaiah had said, "Though your sins be as scarlet, they shall be white as snow; though they be red as crimson, they shall be as wool" (1:18). The sin-scarlet Samaritan woman with five husbands became the evangelist of Samaria, and to the woman taken in the act of adultery Jesus said, "Neither do I condemn thee: go thy way; . . . sin no more" (John 8:11). But such forgiveness is based on genuine heartfelt repentance. "Circumcise yourselves to the Lord, and take away the foreskins of your heart" is another way of saying, "Your repentance must be to the uttermost of your spiritual possibilities." There must be a change in attitude, a change in loyalties, a change in outlook, and a change in the pattern of living. This and only this is repentance. True repentance is the beginning of a life-long process of taking God's attitude toward sin.

Though she was polluted with the filth of false lovers (3:1), though she was ashamed as the thief when he is found (2:26), though the noble vine had turned into the degenerate plant of a strange vine (2:21), though she was gadding about from one foreign alliance to another (2:36), and though she was lying down in shame and covered by confusion (3:25), Judah might yet be healed. God's love is eternal, and his mercy will pardon and cleanse.

In the *Idylls of the King* Tennyson tells of Guinevere. She had sinned against the love of her husband, Arthur. In shame because of her sin she fled to the Holy House of Malmesbury, and Arthur followed her. Tennyson has Arthur say these words:

> Yet think not that I come to urge thy crimes;
> I did not come to curse thee, Guinevere,
> I, whose vast pity almost makes me die
> To see thee, laying there thy golden head,
> My pride in happier summers, at my feet.
> . . . My doom is, I love thee still.

Jehovah still loved Judah and would receive Judah if she would come to him.

3

Blow the Trumpet!

The next section, 4:5 to 6:30, may be entitled "The Foe from the North." This also is one of Jeremiah's earlier oracles and was delivered during the same general period as 2:1 to 4:4. The section consists of a number of short poems and a few verses in prose. The prophet was warning the people with a note of alarm that judgment was coming from the north. The seething pot was about to boil over, and destruction was coming in the person of a foreign invader. Although it is clear that this entire passage is one unit, it is practically impossible to find a stabilized outline. The "boy preacher" was convinced that the judgment of a righteous God upon a sinful people was inevitable. He uttered sharp words of warning and with throbs of emotion begged the people to "gird thee with sackcloth, and wallow thyself in ashes" (6:26) as a symbol of their repentance.

Who was this "foe from the north"? There have been two main schools of thought. Some have maintained that Jeremiah referred to Babylon. This message was delivered close to 626 B.C. The young prophet looked out upon international politics and saw Babylon's star rising in the East. He foresaw Babylon's defeating Assyria in 605 at the Battle of Carchemish and becoming the master of the great Assyrian empire.

He saw Babylon's coming from the north and east and swooping down upon Judah.

The other school of thought identifies the northern foe with the Scythians. This group of barbarians lived in the saddle and might be compared with the Huns and the Vandals of a later generation. This is a popular view among scholars today. According to parallel historical material, the Scythians were carrying on raiding expeditions at this very time. They came down the western coast of Palestine and visited Egypt. Much of the language in Jeremiah's oracle fits the Scythians.

Of course, there is a way to reconcile both schools of thought. Jeremiah began his ministry with a profound conviction that judgment was coming from the north. God had revealed this to him in his inaugural vision. At that time the northern foe threatening Judah was the Scythians. Thus Jeremiah's preaching referred to the invader in language that fit these barbarians. Later, time proved that the real foe from the north was to be Babylon. On the other hand, the great reformation under Josiah in 621 could have been that which caused Jehovah to spare Judah from the Scythians while later, when the people returned to evil under Jehoiakim and Zedekiah, Jehovah raised up a new foe, Babylon.

The complete solution will probably never be known. But this passage is profitable because of the light it sheds on God's attitude toward sin. There is a definite relationship in the divine economy between sin and judgment. The moral law has always declared that sin and death are inevitable equivalents. This section is built around three main thoughts.

Hide Thyself!

This command was given to the people in order that they might find protection and safety from the northern invader.

Destruction was on the way. "Blow ye the trumpet. . . . Assemble yourselves . . . go into the fortified cities. . . . A lion is gone up from his thicket, and a destroyer of nations . . . is on his way, he is gone forth from his place, to make thy land desolate, that thy cities be laid waste, without inhabitant" (4:5, 7).

Old Testament scholars put this type of writing in a special category. When divine intervention is of a catastrophic and cataclysmic nature, it is called "apocalyptic." Most of the canonical prophets have a section of this type in their prophecies. The young preacher saw the invader and pictured him graphically. "He shall come up as clouds, and his chariots shall be as the whirlwind; his horses are swifter than eagles" (4:13). "Behold, a people cometh from the north country; and a great nation shall be stirred up from the uttermost parts of the earth. They lay hold on bow and spear; they are cruel, and have no mercy; their voice roareth like the sea, and they ride upon horses, every one set in array, as a man to the battle, against thee" (6:22–23). The young prophet saw the invader at work. He was to be "a hot wind from the bare heights in the wilderness" (4:11). The wind would not be to fan or to cleanse but would be a full wind of judgment. The invader "shall thoroughly glean the remnant of Israel as a vine" (6:9).

He also saw the whole city fleeing from the noise of the horsemen and bowmen; the people were going into the thickets and climbing upon the rocks: every city would be forsaken, with not a man dwelling therein (4:29). He heard the voice of Judah gasping for breath because of judgment; her wails were as agonizing as those of a woman in the pangs of childbirth (4:31). When the invader came, Judah would be helpless. Her hands would wax feeble; anguish would take hold of her people. They were warned not to go into the field, for the sword of the enemy would be on every side (6:24–25). The nation was doomed. "A lion out of the forest shall slay them, a wolf of the evenings shall destroy them, a leopard shall watch against their cities; everyone that goeth out thence shall be torn in pieces" (5:6).

At the same time Jeremiah was warning Judah with these dreadful pictures of the coming invasion, a contemporary, Zephaniah, was also preaching in Judah. The theme of his three-chapter book is "The Day of the Lord." The burden of his message is very similar to this portion of Jeremiah's ministry. It is highly probable that the Scythian threat forms the historical background for Zephaniah's ministry. He shared Jeremiah's alarm for Judah's safety:

> I will utterly consume all things from off the face of the ground, saith Jehovah. I will consume man and beast; I will consume the birds of the heaven; and the fishes of the sea . . . I will cut off man from off the face of the ground. . . . The great day of Jehovah. . . . is a day of wrath, a day of trouble and distress, a day of wasteness and desolation, a day of darkness and gloominess, a day of clouds and thick darkness, a day of the trumpet and alarm, against the fortified cities, and against the high battlements (1:2–3, 14–16).

Jeremiah portrayed further the condition of the land when the northern force had done its worst. The land would be without form and void; the heavens would have no light. The mountains would tremble, the birds of the heavens would have fled, the fruitful place would become a wilderness, the cities would be broken down, the whole land would be desolate, and the heavens above would be black. The food would be seized by the conquering hordes. "They shall eat up thy harvest, and thy bread, which thy sons and thy daughters should eat; they shall eat up thy flocks and thy herds; they shall eat up thy vines and thy fig-trees" (5:17).

Behind all of this was the prophetic certainty that God was acting. Just as Amos was convinced that every effect has a cause (Amos 3:4–8), so Jeremiah kept before the people that it was Jehovah who would "bring a nation upon you from far . . . a mighty nation . . . an ancient nation, a nation whose language thou knowest not, neither understandest what they say" (5:15).

Judgment was coming. It was declared in Judah and published in Jerusalem. Flee for safety! Hide thyself!

Examine Thyself!

A second thought runs through these Scythian songs. This judgment upon the people was because of their sin. Some have avowed, without much deep thought, "It pays to serve God, but it doesn't pay to sin." This is far from true. Sin does pay, but it pays off in currency that is minted in the coffers of hell. The burden of Jeremiah's message was that Judah's sins had taken good things from her and her iniquities had turned away the blessings of a fertile land (5:25).

Judah needed to examine herself. She had been rebellious (4:17). Evil thoughts lodged within her (4:14). Her wickedness was that of a bitter heart (4:18). As a cage is full of birds, so were the people's houses full of deceit. They had become great and had waxed rich because they overpassed in deeds of wickedness, pleaded not the cause of the fatherless, and judged not the right of the needy (5:27–28).

Judah's people were a foolish people and without understanding (4:22); they had eyes and saw not, ears and heard not (5:21). Their ear was uncircumcised, and they could not hearken. The word of Jehovah had become unto them a reproach. They had no delight in it (6:10). They were so filled with abominations that they had lost their shame and were unable to blush (6:15).

Judah had no understanding of spiritual values. Her sottish children (4:22) had forsaken the true God and sworn by them that are no gods (5:7). They were wise to do evil, but to do good they had no knowledge (4:22). The transgressions of Judah were many, and their backslidings were increased (5:6). God had stricken them, but they were not grieved; he had consumed them, but they refused to receive instruction. They made their faces harder than a rock; they refused to return (5:3). God had set watchmen over them, "saying, Hearken to the sound of the trumpet; but they said, We will not hearken" (6:17).

Judah's religious leaders had led the people astray. From the least of Judah's inhabitants to the greatest "every one is given to covetousness; and from the prophet even unto the priest every one dealeth falsely" (6:13). The false prophets, with their superficial optimism, had shouted, "Peace, peace; when there is no peace" (6:14). Because the prophets had failed to hold high the banner of God's holiness, the house of Israel and the house of Judah had dealt treacherously. "They have belied the Lord, and said, It is not he; neither shall evil come upon us; neither shall we see sword or famine: and the prophets shall become wind, and the word is not in them" (5:12–13, AV). The prophets prophesied falsely, and the priests followed the guidance of the prophets. Both groups compromised moral principles in order that they might "scrape the money" into their own pockets. These official representatives of God were pleased with the situation, and the people were well content that this sinister alliance should work its baneful will. "My people love to have it so" (5:31).

Jeremiah was pessimistic about Judah's moral condition. He was close to cynicism. He had almost come to the place of doubting the existence of even one righteous man. The first part of chapter 5 suggests the story of Diogenes' searching Athens with a lamp in his hands as he tried in vain to find a truthful man. Jeremiah declared that if one man could be found in the streets of Jerusalem that executed judgment and looked for the truth, Jehovah would pardon the city (5:1). After searching without success, the prophet decided that these people were too poor and, therefore, too foolish to know the way of God. They refused to receive instruction and "made their faces harder than a rock" because they were of a lower class (5:3–4). The fifth verse pictures Jeremiah as he decided to turn and seek righteousness among the men of higher social strata. Here, too, he failed. The "up and outs" were as bad if not worse than the "down and outs."

The nation's moral bankruptcy was reflected in the destruction of the sacredness of the marriage vows. In the ease and luxury of the day the "fed horses . . . neighed after his neighbor's wife" (5:8). As a fountain cast out her waters over the land, Judah's sins were overflowing cesspools. Violence and destruction in the land produced grief and wounds in the spiritual life of the nation (6:7).

God was weary of withholding his judgment. How could God pardon a people who had forsaken him and had sworn by gods that are no gods? Jehovah had fed his people to the full, but their ingratitude, sharper than the winter's wind and keener than a serpent's tooth, was expressed in their adultery and in their assembling by troops in the houses of harlots (5:7). How can a righteous God withhold himself? Must he not because of the very nature of his character visit judgment and avenge his soul on such a nation? Speaking for God, the prophet cried, "Hear, O earth: behold, I will bring evil upon this people, even the fruit of their thoughts. . . . Like as ye have forsaken me, and served foreign gods in your land, so shall ye serve strangers in a land that is not yours" (6:19; 5:19). The people had rejected Jehovah and "refuse silver shall men call them, because Jehovah hath rejected them" (6:30). If Judah wished to know why judgment was coming, let her examine herself and see the spiritual vacuum of her national and individual life.

Wash Thyself!

Was there any hope for Judah? Could there be any deliverance, or is the message one of unconditional doom? In the light of God's love, to ask that question is but to answer it. The fundamental fact of Hebrew prophecy was the conditional element. God's threatened judgments were always to come *unless* the people repented. God's promised blessings were always upon the condition that the people respond to his claims upon their lives. "Ye have seen what I did unto the Egyptians, and how I bore you on eagles' wings, and brought you unto myself. Now therefore, if ye will obey my voice indeed, and keep my covenant, then ye shall be mine own possession from among all peoples" (Ex. 19:4–5). Jehovah spoke later in what Kirkpatrick has called the fundamental verses in the Old Testament concerning prophecy: "At what instant I shall speak concerning a nation, and concerning a kingdom, to pluck up and to break down and to destroy it; if that nation, concerning which I have spoken, turn from their evil, I will repent of the evil that I thought to do unto them" (Jer. 18:7–8). In the days of Solomon, Jehovah said, "If my people, who are called by my name, shall humble themselves, and pray, and seek my face, and turn from their wicked

41

ways; then will I hear from heaven, and will forgive their sin, and will heal their land" (2 Chron. 7:14). Isaiah promised and warned, "If ye be willing and obedient, ye shall eat the good of the land: but if ye refuse and rebel, ye shall be devoured with the sword" (1:19–20).

Jeremiah was not a prophet of doom. In fact, none of the prophets were convinced that Judah's case was hopeless. To condemn sin was their lot, and they did not halt or stammer in doing it. But underlying every message was a hope for healing. Even Amos and Zephaniah, who more than any other prophets saw the terrors of the Day of the Lord, saw beyond judgment to the blessing and happiness of the people who would seek the Lord.

Where was Judah's help? It was not in continuing to seek the favor of her false gods. The opiate of worldly thrills and glamorous garments would not turn back the purposes of God in judgment. "Though thou clothest thyself with scarlet, though thou deckest thee with ornament of gold, though thou enlargest thine eyes with paint, in vain dost thou make thyself fair; thy lovers despise thee, they seek thy life" (4:30).

Furthermore, it was not in the attempted bribery of God through burnt offerings. Ceremony has its place in religion, but ritual is no substitute for righteousness. God will not accept the deeds of men's hands in lieu of the devotion of their hearts. "To what purpose cometh there to me frankincense from Sheba, and the sweet cane from a far country? your burnt offerings are not acceptable, nor your sacrifices pleasing unto me" (6:20).

But Jeremiah's message was not merely negative. He had a positive solution. His twofold task involved an affirmative approach. It contained three steps:

Judah must wash herself from wickedness. Jeremiah may have been a prophet of spiritual religion with a touch of the mystic, but he never soft-pedaled the doctrines of sin and repentance. To him sin was treason against God's moral law and contempt in God's court of justice. Before man could be in proper relationship with a righteous God, he must do some straight thinking about his sinful state. Perhaps Jeremiah thought of David, who prayed in his great Psalm that God would purge him with hyssop and create within him a clean heart, when he warned that any other way of salvation was a vain thought lodging within and that only as Judah would "wash thy heart from wickedness" could disaster be averted (4:14).

Judah must be instructed. Salvation is more, however, than repentance. It is a resolve to learn God's will and to seek diligently to follow it. This is not inconsistent with salvation by grace through faith but, on the contrary, is an approach to the real meaning of faith. The highest concept of faith is that of a living and vital relationship with God. It is based upon the acceptance of certain historical and intellectual facts, but it goes beyond the mere learning of facts. It is learning of the Lord (Matt. 11:29), learning his statutes (Psalm 119:71), learning to fear him (Deut. 4:10), ceasing to do evil, learning to do well (Isa. 1:16–17), and learning to maintain good works (Titus 3:14). The promise of Jesus concerning the Holy Spirit was, "He shall teach you all things" (John 16:13). Let Judah learn as she wills to do his will.

Judah must go back to the old-time religion. If Judah would have rest for her soul. she must find it in the faith of her fathers. The religion of Hezekiah could not save her, but a religion like that of Hezekiah could bring peace as it brought deliverance in the Assyrian crisis of Isaiah's day.

There is a difference between living on "borrowed religion" and profiting by the spiritual example of those who have gone before. Our own nation today is a striking example of a people who need to get back to fundamentals in religious life. There is a great vacuum in our spiritual lives that reflects itself in our home, business, and social lives. It will be changed only by returning to some old-fashioned convictions concerning right and wrong. A morally color-blind generation has allowed the black and white of wickedness and righteousness to fade into a dull gray of spiritual indifference. The words of Jeremiah to Judah are relevant to our national life: "Thus saith Jehovah, Stand ye in the ways and see, and ask for the old paths, where is the good way; and walk therein, and ye shall find rest for your souls" (6:16).

The God of Jeremiah was the God of Hosea, who desired mercy and not sacrifice and the knowledge of himself more than burnt offerings (Hos. 6:6). He was the God of Amos, who insisted that justice run down as waters and righteousness as a mighty stream (Amos 5:24). He was the God of Micah, whose requirement was that a man do justly, love kindness, and walk humbly with his God (Mic. 6:8). He was the God of Isaiah, who in the days of Hezekiah and Sennacherib spared Jerusalem when, as Byron put it,

> . . . the might of the Gentile, unsmote by the sword,
> . . . melted like snow in the glance of the Lord!

Let Judah return to her God who in yesteryear sent his angel to smite the enemy. How can God pardon his children who have forsaken him? Only as they wash themselves from wickedness (4:14), become instructed in his will (6:8), and turn to the old paths and find the good way (6:16).

4

When the Bubble Bursts

With the close of the sixth chapter of Jeremiah the chronological arrangement of the book ceases. Possibly Jeremiah is a collection of a number of rolls, each of which possessed logical and perhaps chronological arrangement within itself. These rolls existed and circulated independently. When the book of Jeremiah was placed in its permanent form, one roll apparently was added to another without any attempt to synchronize them with reference to dates of composition and delivery. The first roll contains an account of the call and early prophecies of Jeremiah. This first division is easily discernible, but an analysis of the rest of the book is not so simple.

It is necessary to gather material from several sections of the book for a consideration of the next period in Jeremiah's life. This chapter will deal with the ministry of Jeremiah from the discovery of the law book in the Temple to the death of Jehoahaz, who ruled for three months in Jerusalem after the death of Josiah. This period pictures a prophet preaching in his home town, persecuted by his kinsmen, popular with the masses, perplexed when popular religion failed, and finally perceiving the truth that spiritual religion is deeper than, and not to be confused with, national pride and legal obedience.

Preaching (11:1–8; 17:19–27)

In the year 621 B.C. there occurred an event and began a movement which made a distinct division in Josiah's reign. It was also of profound significance for the future of Jewish religion and for the career of Jeremiah. According to second Chronicles, the king had made minor reforms in his youth, but in the eighteenth year of his reign Josiah's zeal for religion inspired him to make a thorough purge of the land and the Temple (2 Chron. 34).

As the Temple was being cleansed, there was found a book called by the chronicler "the book of the law of Jehovah given by Moses." It is the general verdict of Old Testament scholarship that this was the book of Deuteronomy. The discovery of this document began a series of reforms which swept the entire land of Judah. Religious customs and observances which had been neglected for years were resumed by order of the king.

It is difficult to realize the effect this reformation would have on the small villages outside Jerusalem. Skinner gives us a vivid picture of the results of this reformation in Jeremiah's home town. It may be that in 621 Jeremiah was still living in comparative obscurity in the little village.

. . . In the spring of that year, a rumour reaches the village of the discovery in the Temple of an ancient law-book, said to be that of Moses, which had caused the gravest concern to the king because of the glaring disparity between its requirements and the existing state of things in matters religious and moral. This is speedily followed by a summons to the local elders to a great national convention at Jerusalem at the approaching Passover season. When the delegates return they have a thrilling story to tell—of a Passover such as had never been observed in Israel before, of a Solemn League and Covenant entered into by the king and the heads of the people to make the newly found law the basis of public religion, and to extirpate everything inconsistent with it, of a cleansing of the Temple from idolatrous emblems, the ejection of sacred prostitutes and the whole crew of diviners, astrologers and wizards from the Temple precincts, and many other startling demonstrations of reforming and iconoclastic zeal. Enough already to rouse the misgivings of all lovers of the old order in Anathoth! By and by the village is visited by a royal commission with sufficient force to overpower resistance; the edict proclaiming the new covenant is read, and then the work of destruction is done on the local *Bāmā* or "high place," where sacrifice to Yahwe is no longer to be permitted. Something like this must have taken place at every township throughout the country in that memorable year.[1]

There have been two chief views among scholars concerning Jeremiah's attitude toward the Deuteronomic Reformation. One group has maintained that Jeremiah was a zealous advocate of the legal religion, while another group has contended that from the beginning the prophet saw the superficial character of such reforms and had no part in their enforcement. The truth probably lies somewhere between these two extremities. The evidence seems convincing that Jeremiah supported the reforms at their inception. But the evidence is equally persuasive that Jeremiah rose above the legalistic approach and came to a clear conception of spiritual religion.

Two passages give us a picture of Jeremiah as he preached the message of the covenant. One section (11:1–8) shows Jeremiah as he pleaded with the people to observe the words of the covenant. He based God's command for obedience

47

upon his deliverance of the people from the iron furnace of Egyptian oppression. They were to obey in order that God should bless them in accordance with his promise to their fathers. Jeremiah was commanded to proclaim these words throughout the cities of Judah and the streets of Jerusalem. As the young prophet toured the rural sections, he pronounced a curse upon those who refused to obey all the requirements of the covenant and warned of the Lord's purpose to bring upon the people all the threatenings of the covenant if they continued to refuse to incline their ears and walk in obedience.

The other section which dates from this period of covenant preaching is found in 17:19-27. This passage is called "The Sabbath Day Discourse" and is a message concerning the proper observance of the sabbath with a strong appeal for strict conformity to the rigid requirements of legal obedience. It is interesting to note that as late as the time of Nehemiah this message was influencing some people's thought. This is evidenced by a passage (Neh. 13:15-22) which shows a strong affinity to Jeremiah's message. In fact, the resemblance is so significant that many modern critical scholars contend that Jeremiah is not the author of 17:19-27. They insist a prophet contemporaneous with Nehemiah wrote or delivered the message under Jeremiah's name and that it was thus incorporated into one of the later editions of the book. The evidence, however, when properly investigated and evaluated, does not justify the conclusion of these sceptical scholars.

This message concerning the sabbath day is important. Although a mere legal approach is not a sufficient answer, there is a definite need in our day for the Christian sabbath to be hallowed and reverenced. The proper observance of the Lord's Day, we must realize, is not a mere end in itself. The attitude toward the sabbath is indicative of an entire concept of religion. Personal conviction concerning the Lord's Day, even in our time, is a good indication of personal convictions in all phases of Christian morality. Jeremiah reasoned that if the people of his day had enough religion to keep the sabbath, they would also have enough piety to obey God in all areas of their life. Orelli says,

This passage shows how the prophet, with all the inwardness and spirituality of his conception of God's kingdom, yet regarded the chief outward commands given by God in the old covenant as inalienable, and desired them to be strictly carried out for the people's good. . . . But the Sabbath-law was then, as still later in exilian days . . . a touchstone of the people's obedience, of its entire religious attitude to God.[2]

The discussion of Jeremiah's attitude toward the sabbath will not be complete unless we say a word about our own generation. One of the best books written on the subject is a work by W. O. Carver entitled *Sabbath Observance*. Approaching the subject with a recognition of the necessity of constructive principles, yet clinging devotedly to some basic convictions, he says, "*Keep it holy* . . . That is the beginning of true Sabbath observance. . . . The first question should not be, What must I do and what may I not do? Rather, How may I make the most of this day for my Lord and his purposes; for my own life and its completeness; for the church and its meaning? "Keep it holy" in the sense of guarding it for its purpose and uses."[3]

Persecution (11:18 to 12:6)

Next in the chronological development of Jeremiah's ministry is a section which deals with the manner in which his preaching was received by the people of his home town. This passage is a striking illustration of the later words of Jesus that "a prophet is not without honor, save in his own country" (Mark 6:4).

Jeremiah was on a preaching tour urging the people to adopt the principles of Josiah's reform movement. One of the chief planks in the Deuteronomic platform was the establishment of worship at a central sanctuary and the abolition of the local worship places throughout the small towns and rural sections.

This was not a new problem in the religious life of the people. Jereboam I had won his way into the hearts of the Northern Kingdom by setting up sanctuaries at Dan and Bethel in competition with the one in the Temple at Jerusalem (1 Kings 12:27–29). When Rabshakeh, propaganda agent for Sennacherib, was attempting to persuade the people to surrender Jerusalem, he sought to arouse the prejudice of the common people against Hezekiah by reminding them that it was Hezekiah who had removed the local worship places and enforced centralized worship (Isa. 36:7).

There was still another sore spot in the hearts of the people of Anathoth. This little town was the home of Abiathar's descendants. For years this priestly family had held resentment against the descendants of Zadok. They had never ceased to maintain that they were the ones who should be at Jerusalem ministering about the sacred things of the Temple. It was at the accession of Solomon to the throne that Abiathar and his family had been banished to Anathoth and Zadok made chief priest in his stead (1 Kings 2:26). Now here was a young upstart of a preacher telling them to discontinue worship at their home when they were indeed the historical succession of true priestly function. Thus would be the reasoning of the men of Anathoth, and this section shows their desire to kill the prophet. One wonders if their position was not somewhat comparable to the worshipers of Diana in Ephesus on Paul's third missionary journey. Jeremiah's preaching the centralization of worship at Jerusalem could have meant havoc for the religious trade in connection with the sacrifices, even as Paul's preaching in a later day at Ephesus was to endanger the business of the craftsmen who made silver images to be used in the worship of Diana. Even in our own day of organized Christianity there is too many times a close connection, sometimes closer than we realize, between the religion and the income produced as a by-product of the religious program. It is sometimes difficult to discover for which the zeal is greater. One writer facetiously paraphrases Acts 19:27: "These men are ruining our business, and incidentally it's hurting our religion, too."

This entire section forms one unit. The first division (11:18–23) relates how the Lord gave Jeremiah knowledge of a plot against his life (vv. 18–20) and then tells of Jehovah's declaration of punishment against those who plotted against Jeremiah (vv. 21–23). The second division (12:1–6) represents Jeremiah as complaining to Jehovah because of the prosperity of the wicked and demanding that they be visited with vengeance. He was rebuked for his impatience and told, in the words of Charles Jefferson, "Cheer up, for the worst is yet to come." Greater trials and heartache await the prophet in the years ahead.

The account of the plot against the prophet and his reaction to it is a part of the material in Jeremiah's prophecies called "The Confessions of Jeremiah." This subject will be discussed more fully in chapter 11 in connection with a related topic.

Popularity

The preacher was not so ill-treated in other places as in Anathoth. In fact, it seems that he received an opposite reception in other sections of the land. At least, this is the only satisfactory explanation for one peculiar fact about the prophecies of Jeremiah.

The chronology of the events in Jeremiah's life present a serious problem. There is a period of silence for about thirteen years between the great reformation in 621 and the death of Josiah in 608. Raymond Calkins expresses the opinion of many when he avows that there is not a single prophecy in the book which can be assigned with any degree of certainty to that period.

There have been several suggestions offered to explain this silent period, but C. F. Kent presents the one which appears most probable: The decade which followed the Deuteronomic Reformation appears to have been the happiest and most prosperous in Judah's stormy history. For a time the commands of the book of the covenant were applied in the lives of the people. Even Jeremiah was happy because they were following faithfully the guidance of the code. But as time passed, the prophet saw that this legislated and popular religion was developing into a superficial legalism.[4]

If this explanation be accepted, then the matter is clear. Jeremiah uttered no oracles against the sins of the land because in his opinion "the millennium had come." Everyone was on the bandwagon of religious reform. His preaching tour had been a success. The people had righteousness—at least a form of righteousness—and there was no need to denounce their sins or decry the condition of the land. The country had escaped the foe by turning back to the old paths.

Let any nation beware when religion is too popular. Let any religious group carefully re-examine its standards when membership in it is too sought after. Organized religion should heed the words of, and bear constantly in mind, Cowper's warning,

> O Popular Applause! what heart of man
> Is proof against thy sweet, seducing charms?

and Wordsworth's

> I have been nourished by the sickly food
> Of popular applause.

and Milton's

> Honor, glory, and popular praise,
> Rocks whereon greatest men have oftest wrecked.

In his *Moral Essays* Pope speaks of "the itch of vulgar praise." It is this itch that constitutes one of the greatest temptations to modern Christianity. In *A Faith for Tough Times*, Dr. Fosdick speaks challengingly:

Church membership in this nation is at an all-time high. Never, in recent years, has so large a proportion of our population been inside the churches. Church attendance is apparently increasing, and 95 per cent of our people, poll-takers say, believe in God. Yet look at us! In one realm after another of personal and public behavior we do not give the impression to ourselves or to anybody else that we are really a Christian people.[5]

The religion of our Lord was never meant to win a popularity contest. This is not to say that every impetus of religious fervor is hypocrisy, but it is to say with Robert Browning that "praise is deeper than the lips" and to affirm that the relevance of that statement for our day is that heart piety is more needed in God's kingdom than lip service.

Perplexity

We do not know how long this period of popular religion continued. Perhaps Jeremiah began early to have doubts and misgivings concerning this spiritual bubble that was causing the people to be wise in their own religious conceits and complacently comfortable with their perfunctory obedience to the mechanics of legal religion. But those doubts could easily be rationalized. Judah was doing well. Surely God was pleased with this religious fervor. Why should the preacher interfere with the program?

This is always the pattern of a person-centered religious program. The bubble of activity gets bigger, and the person around whom the movement is centered continues to encourage the program. Consciously or unconsciously, the people feed the ego of the leader, and the leader reciprocates by being perfectly willing to be the object of such worship and adoration.

Something like this must have happened in Judah. Outwardly the land was in the midst of a great revival. There was much religious activity. But inwardly there was little spiritual progress. The people's zeal was more for national glory than for humility of character. They had become filled with personal pride because of their religious reforms. The worship of Jehovah had turned into the worship of Josiah.

Then one day the bubble burst! In the year 608 Pharaoh Necho of Egypt was on his way to Carchemish. Assyria and Babylon were about to engage in a battle there that would decide who was to rule the world. Scholars are still divided as to which country Necho planned to assist. The probability is, however, that Egypt wanted to see the destruction of her old enemy, Assyria. Intoxicated with the idea that Jehovah was his unconditional ally, Josiah endeavored to halt Necho's northern march. The book of 2 Chronicles (35:20–25) tells that Josiah was killed at Megiddo and that all the people, including Jeremiah, wept for the king. This incident and the period of confusion in Judah which followed it serves as the historical background for the material in 8:14 to 9:1.

The bubble of popular religion had burst. Judah did not have the internal resources to carry her through the crisis. The person died, and the person-centered religion crumbled into dust.

Perception

It was then that Jeremiah began to perceive a great truth. He would develop it further in his subsequent ministry. Religion, he began to see, is deeper than creed, form, or institution. Even good works with the hands will be unacceptable unless the heart is touched by God's loving spirit. There is a great difference between legislated righteousness and spiritual devotion.

As long as Josiah reigned in Jerusalem the people were confident that Jehovah was present, too. But Josiah was dead. The people must have another king in order that Jehovah's presence in Jerusalem might be personified through their ruler. The people placed Jehoahaz on the throne, but Necho carried him into Egypt to die in exile after reigning only three months. The Egyptian ruler then placed Jehoiakim on Judah's throne, and Judah's dark days began.

What was happening to Jeremiah during this time? He

was revising his theological outlook. He was reinterpreting his faith. He was listening to God's voice rather than to the praise of the people. Religion is not ceremony or form. It is an affair of the heart, a spiritual fellowship with a God of righteousness and love. The bubble of Judah's superficial religion had burst, but with it had come a deepening of the prophet's religious insight. The days of Jehoiakim's rule would be dark and discouraging, but Jeremiah would "cleave to the sunnier side of doubt" and be fortified by a "faith beyond the forms of faith."

5
What's Worse Than No Religion?

In one of his essays Ralph Waldo Emerson asks the stimulating question, "What greater calamity can fall upon a nation than the loss of worship?" The normal answer is that there could be no greater tragedy than a people without an altar, but this section of Jeremiah (7:1 to 8:3; 26:1–24) deals with a condition that was in many ways worse than no religion. It is the picture of a people who were inoculated with a false concept of worship which made them complacently immune to real religion.

Students of Jeremiah are united in designating this material as "The Temple Sermon," although there is some disagreement as to how far this discourse continues. Perhaps the most logical idea is that the message goes through the first three verses of the eighth chapter. There is a somewhat parallel passage in chapter 26, and most scholars take the position that the two sections represent the same occasion and the same sermon. The difference, it is maintained, is to be found in the purpose of writing. The material in 7:1 to 8:3 is the record of a sermon preached by Jeremiah, while 26:1–24 contains a condensation of the sermon accompanied by a historical account showing the effect of the message upon the people.

The fact that the two passages are widely separated in the book should not militate against their being accepted as the same sermon and the same occasion since one is in a section of prophetic discourses while the other is in a section of historical material. The similarities are inescapable. Both sermons took place by the specific command of Jehovah. Both occurred in the gate of the Temple. The subject is the same, an invitation to repentance is given in both, and an identical punishment is threatened. The fate of Shiloh (1 Sam. 4:9–22) would be the fate of this people if they failed to heed the prophetic warning.

The date which should be assigned to the Temple sermon is the early part of the reign of Jehoiakim. Skinner points out that one of the few tangible and enduring results of Josiah's reforms was the centralization of worship at the Temple in Jerusalem. The tragic truth was, however, that this love for the Temple had degenerated into a kind of fetish superstition. One is reminded at this point of Isaiah's continued emphasis on the indestructibility of Zion. Perhaps the people of Jeremiah's day were still influenced strongly by Isaiah's teaching.

Jeremiah had been watching this growing superstition and saw the deadening effect it was having upon the spiritual development of the people. Faith cannot be mere superstition and be a faith of spiritual fellowship and vitality. Edmund Burke once described superstition as "the religion of feeble minds," and Joubert asserts that "superstition is the only religion of which base souls are capable."

It was when the Battle of Megiddo and the death of Josiah brought a national crisis that Jeremiah saw clearly Judah's lack of real religion. She had a superficial righteousness clothed with formalism and bound up with a patriotic zeal. The result of this combination was a shallow superstition about God rather than a living fellowship with God. In short, Judah's worship, consisting of ceremonies and chants, was so perverted that it was worse than no religion.

It is easier to win a sin-stained individual to faith in Christ than to open the blinded eyes of an unconverted church member to his spiritual poverty. It was to a church that Jesus spoke through John, but the message is relevant to an individual as well: "Because thou sayest, I am rich, and have gotten riches, and have need of nothing; and knowest not that thou art the wretched one and miserable and poor and blind and naked: I counsel thee to buy of me gold refined by fire, that thou mayest become rich; and white garments, that thou mayest clothe thyself, and that the shame of thy nakedness be not made manifest; and eyesalve to anoint thine eyes, that thou mayest see" (Rev. 3:17-18). The teaching of Jesus concerning the kingdom of God seems to have been accepted by the harlots and prostitutes before it was received by the scribes and Pharisees. This was not because his message compromised with immorality but because there is something worse than having no religion—having the wrong kind.

The greatest teachings of this passage of Scripture, however, are not negative. There are to be found in it some positive truths about worship. They have negative corollaries, to be sure, but more will be accomplished, in any field, when the positive virtue is emphasized than when the negative fallacy is condemned. William Gladstone once said, "To be engaged in opposing wrong affords, under the conditions of our mental constitution, but a slender guarantee for being right." The remainder of this discussion will not merely be a condemnation of Judah's shortcoming but an effort to discover the elements of true worship.

Character

The Scottish preacher, James Stewart, speaks of religion and character as "God-intended alliances." This is not to deny that the Christian experience begins as a rescue from sin's penalties through repentance toward God and faith in the Lord Jesus Christ. The emphasis here, however, is that the only kind of Christianity worthy of the name of our Lord is that religion and that worship which is related to personal behavior and results in the raising of moral standards. Any worship which is lacking here fails at the most vital point.

This was exactly where Judah's religion missed the mark. Her worship was not related to her daily living. Jeremiah asked a heart-searching question: "Will ye steal, murder, and commit adultery, and swear falsely, and burn incense unto Baal, and walk after other gods . . . and come and stand before me in this house, which is called by my name, and say, We are delivered; that ye may do all these abominations?" (7:9–10). In the language of our own day the prophet would be asking, "Will you be a regular attender at the worship services of your church, meeting all of the external and perfunctory requirements of institutionalized religion, and yet go from the sanctuary unaffected and unchanged in your daily living?" Worship which fails to produce character is not only without value but it is also blasphemous to a God of righteousness and holiness.

The type of worship in which Judah was engaged is dangerous to the best interests of a nation. The people of Jeremiah's day had allowed their warped conception of worship to issue forth in religious observance which had become an opiate, "dulling and deadening the spiritual sense." Instead of serving as a constraining force for higher moral and ethical development, this type of worship was causing the people to say, "Peace, peace; when there is no peace" (8:11). They were certain that because the altars of the Temple were piled high with offerings the moral and spiritual life of the people had reached a corresponding maturity. This was not only a false but also a dangerous assumption. This approach to worship appears to support the cynicism of Emerson, who declared, "God builds his temples in the heart on the ruins of churches and religion." Those who love the churches of the Lord, however, can never agree with this Unitarian thinker. They prefer to invest themselves and their efforts in the church and its program. One cannot correct the shortcomings of an institution by leaving it; this approach is as easy as it is selfish. There is enough truth, however, in Emerson's cryptic accusation to force a re-examination of worship. It would be better to agree with Morgan when he says, "The essential value and proof of religion is that of the effect it produces on conduct," and with Swedenborg that "all religion relates to life and the life of religion is to do good."

There is a close relationship between superstition and fear in the patterns and processes of religion. To be sure, fear has its part in religious life. It is the fear of the Lord which is the beginning of wisdom, but it is only the beginning. Spiritual life must have deeper roots than a superstitious fear. Thomas Fuller sensed this when he wrote,

> They that worship God merely from fear,
> Would worship the devil too, if he appear.

It is true, of course, that the original idea of a sanctuary was that of protection. It was at the horns of the altar that

61

the transgressor was safe. The people of Judah, however, were finding a false security in the sanctuary. They could comfortably claim, "We are delivered," as they flocked to the Temple. Judah was overlooking, however, that this word "sanctuary" comes from the same Hebrew root as the words for sanctify, dedicate, and holy. Worship is not complete unless the concept of protection from fear blends into, and gives way to, a growing holiness in character. The people of Judah believed that they could control God, but their real need was to let God control them.

The word "character" has an interesting etymological background. The root from which it comes means a sharp-pointed instrument or engraving tool. The interpretation of this in terms of practical application reveals that it is by character that people make impressions upon the world. A fine instrument improves with use, and character develops into better character as it stands day by day without compromise for Christian principles and Christian integrity. The experience of regeneration is a point, but the development of character is a process. Character is developed by hard struggle. It is not shaped by accident any more than marble is sculptured by puffs of air. H. G. Werner gives this evaluation of character:

Character is that which is found still standing when the crash is over. Character is the moral cash on hand when the creditors close in on life. Character is what you are when no one is around. Character informs your family and friends what you will do under strain or in a crisis. Character is a staff grown strong upon which to lean for well being in old age. Character is what you have been thinking and doing a long time.[1]

The true nature of God is comprehended only as one sees the relationship between spiritual worship and moral demands upon life. There is quite a contrast between the worship of the English sea captain's enjoying his daily reading from the Psalms while the slaves on board his ship were suffering the pangs of hunger and physical pains of rigid disciplinary action and the worship of Isaiah at Uzziah's death as he caught a vision of the thrice holy God of Judah. It was relatively easy for Judah to remember that the Lord was seated upon a throne, but it was a little more difficult for her to hold in mind that before the seraphim spoke of Jehovah's glory, they reminded Isaiah three times of his holiness. The pendulum cannot be swung to the other extremity with the sweeping conclusion that creeds make no difference. Doctrine does matter, and it matters much, but any system of thought or pattern of worship that does not produce Christian character should be re-examined lest it be deficient in its basic affirmation. A religion that fails to make man better in his daily living is useless, no matter how orthodox its form or zealous its activity.

Strength for Life

One of the most universal attacks hurled against the Christian faith by those who are antagonistic to it is that of branding all religion in general, and Christianity in particular, as an escape mechanism by which the worshiper denies reality and builds for himself a world of illusion. This is an accusation which is both unfair and untrue. Observation of the people of seventh-century Judah in their worship would have made it difficult to reach any other conclusion. Judah was using her worship as a crutch to hide her face in ostrich fashion from the mounting crisis both without and within the nation. The phrase "we are delivered" reflects the typically optimistic attitude of the people as they thronged the

Temple for worship. The difference between true worship and that of Judah is that true worship produces an inspiration and a dynamic to strengthen the stakes of life by building internal resources while Judah's worship served only to entrench her in the false confidence that God was the nation's ally no matter what attitude the people took toward the moral demands of Jehovah. There is a vast difference between inner strength because of spiritual resources and overconfidence because of spiritual egotism.

The people had adopted a most satisfying manner of convincing themselves that their worship was pleasing to Jehovah. They would chant the phrase "the Temple of the Lord." It is not certain how many times these words would be repeated, but Jeremiah rebuked their mechanical approach to worship. "Thus saith Jehovah of hosts, the God of Israel, . . . Trust ye not in lying words, saying, The temple of Jehovah, the temple of Jehovah, the temple of Jehovah" (7:3–4). The habit of such repetition was customary in religious ceremonies of the Oriental people. Even in the New Testament the pagan worshipers at Ephesus all with one voice cried out about the space of two hours, "Great is Diana of the Ephesians" (Acts 19:34).

Worship is not the perfunctory chanting of a series of meaningless words, even though they may be good words and may contain an element of truth. Worship is a spiritual fellowship, and when properly interpreted and experienced will bring strength to weakened lives. It was in the Psalms that Old Testament religion was made most truly spiritual. The author of the seventy-third Psalm was giving his spiritual biography. He was disillusioned, discouraged, and nearly despondent. He was rapidly approaching cynicism. As he thought upon what seemed to him to be the inequalities of life and the unfairness of God's rule, it was too painful for him, or as the Hebrew says, "it was labor in my eyes." But a strange and wonderful thing happened. He went into the sanctuary of God. Immediately his outlook and attitude were changed, and the remainder of the Psalm reveals a man of strengthened faith because of his worship experience. The assurance which he received in worship caused him to say, "My flesh . . . faileth; but God is the strength of my heart" (v. 26). Jesus told the Samaritan woman that worship was not to be confused with externals. It is the soul in spiritual communion with God. It is watering that "seed called reverence" which Holmes said he had and which all people possess. Spiritual worship will strengthen every fiber of a person's being.

Any attempted interpretation of the Temple sermon is incomplete unless consideration is given to 7:21–23. In the first of these verses the prophet said sarcastically, "Add your burnt-offerings unto your sacrifices, and eat ye flesh." The accepted teaching here is that burnt offerings and sacrifices had no merit within themselves. The further teaching is that even though they added one type of sacrifice to another in an effort to secure virtue through the sacrificial processes, the cumulative result was the same. The sacrifices were still mere flesh, offered by unclean hands, devoid of any sacred element, atoning force, or sanctifying power. Ritual that did not change man, could not please God.

It is the next verse, however, which raises the difficulty. Jeremiah made a startling statement: "For I spake not unto your fathers, nor commanded them in the day that I brought them out of the land of Egypt, concerning burnt offerings or sacrifices: but this thing I commanded them, saying, Hearken unto my voice, and I will be your God, and ye shall be my people; and walk ye in all the way that I command you, that it may be well with you" (7:22–23).

From the standpoint of critical scholarship this is one of the pivotal verses in the Old Testament. Those who deny that the sacrificial system came from Moses and insist that Deuteronomy was written shortly before 621 B.C. and placed in the Temple for Josiah to discover find here a statement from Jeremiah which allegedly vindicates their position. In fact, this verse, if taken literally, does deny that the sacrificial system is of Mosaic origin. Scholars who accept the documentary hypothesis of the Pentateuch and the developmental theory of Hebrew religion regard this verse as irrefutable proof that their contentions are correct. It is not our intention here to discuss the matter at length inasmuch as we are writing for a different purpose. We should point out, however, that the critical school seems to be doing the same thing with reference to this verse that they criticize the traditionalists and ultra-conservatives for doing with other sections of Scripture. They are taking a strictly literal interpretation and ruling out any other consideration.

As much as one hesitates to disagree with a scholar such as Peake, whose commentary on Jeremiah is probably the best in existence, it does seem that he is unfair in some of his statements regarding this verse. There is, for instance, a strong school of interpretation which lays emphasis on the time element and concludes that God did not give the laws about sacrifice on the *first* day the children of Israel left Egypt. The point is that the moral laws were given first and then the ritualistic requirements. Peake dismisses this interpretation with the phrases "crass piece of Rabbinism" and "obviously absurd." He also rejects the contention of some grammarians that here is an idiom meaning that obedience was the primary and sacrifice the subordinate command. There are still other grammarians who base their interpretation upon a translation which renders "concerning" as "for the sake of," which causes the prophet to declare that God's purpose in giving the sacrificial system was not in order that the sacrifices might be an end in themselves but rather for the people to be taught obedience and discipline. This latter interpretation, however, is perhaps a forced linguistic argument of questionable grammatical accuracy which has not met with wide acceptance among scholars.

These interpretations are interesting and to some extent helpful, but it is not necessary to be a technical scholar in order to understand the prophet's message. Those who accept the historical integrity of the Pentateuch can never agree with the school of thought which contends that Jeremiah was denying the Mosaic origin of the sacrificial system. It seems evident Jeremiah was resorting to a statement of extremity in order to convey his point. He did not expect to be taken literally any more than Jesus did when he said, "If any man cometh unto me, and hateth not his own father, and mother, and wife, and children . . . he cannot be my disciple" (Luke 14:26). It is impossible to compare Jeremiah 7:23 with Exodus 19:4–5 without coming to the definite conclusion that Jeremiah was referring to the words of Moses.

The meaning of this disputed passage is clear unless one has a preconceived opinion. Jeremiah was speaking in the spirit of his predecessors, the great prophets before him. Samuel had said, "To obey is better than sacrifice" (1 Sam. 15:22). Isaiah testified for Jehovah, "What unto me is the multitude of your sacrifices? . . . cease to do evil; learn to do well" (1:11, 17–18). Hosea declared, "I desire goodness, and not sacrifice; and the knowledge of God more than burnt-offerings" (6:6). Micah said that it was not with "thousands of rams, or with ten thousands of rivers of oil . . . but to do justly, and to love kindness, and to walk humbly with thy God" (6:7–8).

The ritualistic worship of ceremonies and sacrifices could not strengthen life; spiritual communion with God brings its own reward. Those who hearken unto the voice of God shall have the assurance that they are his people. Baughman says that they shall taste the "fruits of pure worship in such inner resources as are beyond the natural mind to comprehend."

> But what to those who find? ah! this,
> Nor tongue nor pen can show
> The love of Jesus, what it is
> None but His loved ones know.
>
> BERNARD OF CLAIRVAUX

The True Temple

It remains for the New Testament to give the complete message of the Temple sermon. Paul, though regarded by some as a mere legalist, possessed deep insight into a spiritual application of the gospel. He told the Athenians that God "dwelleth not in temples made with hands" (Acts 17:24). These earthly sanctuaries may symbolize God's presence, but they are still only symbols. The presence of God cannot be limited or circumscribed. To the Jews of Jeremiah's day Jehovah was in Zion, but the new Testament declares "Christ in you, the hope of glory" (Col. 1:27). Jesus insisted that "the kingdom of God is within you" (Luke 17:21), and Paul soared to majestic heights as he triumphantly exclaimed, "Know ye not that ye are a temple of God. . . . The temple of God is holy, and such are ye" (1 Cor. 3:16–17). When men lay hold of this truth and are laid hold of by its relevance to their lives, a spiritual revolution takes place within the inner recesses of their souls. Christians are not to seek safety by entering a temple but by becoming a temple. It is dangerous to be nominally identified with a religious institution unless hearts are in vital contact with the spiritual power of a living relationship with God. One who shelters himself beneath false refuges is as much exposed, perhaps more, to the chilling winds of judgment as one who positionizes himself against a formal acceptance of religion.

A word of caution is necessary here. If we are not careful, we can swing the pendulum too far. Here is a modern man who makes haste to agree with the truth about spiritual religion. He prides himself that he has reached a degree of spiritual maturity that enables him to worship without the crutches of institutionalized religion. Other less developed people, he reasons, may need the support of ecclesiastical props, but he has graduated into the realm of a higher concept. This is a comfortable doctrine and a very popular one. As Elton Trueblood says,

This supposed emancipation from forms and ceremonies can sound very noble as well as advanced and modern. The position gets most of its plausibility from the fact that it bears a superficial resemblance to a great teaching of the gospel, the teaching that God can be known and loved in *any* situation. The spiritual giant has no need of external supports.[2]

The best answer to this is given in the same paragraph:

But the vulgar truth is that most of the people who pass off the wretched cliché about their devotion being to Christianity rather than "churchianity" are not spiritual giants! Men might conceivably have great experiences of God's presence, and their moral need, while getting out of the rough by the seventeenth hole, for nothing is impossible with God, but such an experience is not really *likely* to occur.[3]

Is there not a happy medium, or as Carlyle says, "a point of sweet reasonableness," a way to avoid the "rocks on either side"? Christianity needs to be a personal and vital matter freed from the shackles of mere legal obedience. Yet it cannot be divorced from the sanctuary, the fellowship of believers, and the command of the Lord to make disciples of all nations. Every Christian needs the insight of a mystic combined with the flaming heart of an evangelist. Paul seems to have had this unusual combination found so rarely in one personality. His life and teachings served as an inspiration for Schweitzer to write of "The Mysticism of the Apostle Paul," and yet his passion for the lost could send Moody and Torrey to burn themselves out in personal evangelism.

A minister visited a mission in an underprivileged section of the city to hear a college friend preach. The friend's arrival was delayed because of icy roads, and he did not arrive in time for the service. A substitute took over on a moment's notice. Before the service was completed, most of the people were engaged in emotional excesses. As he was driving home, he remarked to his wife, "If we could take some of the excessive intellectualism at our church to that group and transfer some of their surplus energy and enthusiasm to our members, I think the Lord would be more pleased with both groups."

The emphasis at this point, however, is on the spiritual nature of faith. The best argument for Christianity is still a Christian, and Browning's interpretation of the soul as "God in man" remains relevant for our religious day. A learned professor was once asked, "Can you give me a definition of

Christianity?" Throwing up his hands in despair, he replied, "Oh, never! But I can give you an illustration." And he pointed to Phillips Brooks.

If the true temple is the body of a godly man, there are some basic facts concerning the Christian's attitude toward his body. It is to be used in a manner that will glorify God. Purity at any price should be the ideal of the believer. Byron speaks of this goal in *Childe Harold:* "He had kept the whiteness of his soul, and thus men o'er him wept."

A person's attitude toward his body is a barometer of his relationship to the spiritual values of life. Harry Roberts reminds us that "the body is the temple of the Holy Spirit, and is the means whereby alone the soul can establish relations with the universe"; and Walt Whitman insists, "If anything is sacred the human body is sacred." Paul told the Ephesians that saints are "fellow-citizens . . . built upon the foundation of the apostles and prophets, Christ Jesus himself being the chief corner stone; in whom each several buildings, fitly framed together, groweth into a holy temple in the Lord" (2:19–21). When Jesus warned the Jews, "Destroy this temple, and in three days I will raise it up," John explained, "He spake of the temple of his body" (John 2:19, 21).

Paul might have looked out from the school of Tyrannus, which he was using as headquarters for his teaching and writing in Ephesus, and saw the splendor of the Temple to Diana, the fourth wonder of the ancient world. It was octagonal, measuring 340 by 160 feet. There were 127 pillars 60 feet high made of Parian marble, each erected by a king. The pillars had drums, 20 feet in circumference and 6 feet high, with 8 life-sized figures sculptured on each. The doors of this temple were of carved cypress wood; the roof was

71

cedar. The holy of holies was 70 feet wide and open to the skies. Within a concealed place was the image of Diana, shrouded in thick darkness.

Paul, however, had another concept of a temple. He thought of the human body. He remembered the words of the psalmist, "Thou hast made him a little lower than the angels, and hast crowned him with glory and honour" (Psalm 8:5, AV). He wrote to the Christians at Corinth, "Know ye not that ye are a temple of God" (1 Cor. 3:16). This is the fullest interpretation of a temple. Our bodies are dwelling places for the Spirit of God. We are to "let not sin therefore reign" (Rom. 6:12) in our mortal bodies but rather to live that "Christ shall be magnified" in our bodies "whether by life, or by death" (Phil. 1:20).

6

While the Lights Are Still Burning

There are always three distinct phases in the spiritual regression of a nation or an individual. First, there is a period when the lights burn brightly. Second, there is a time when the lights begin to flicker. Finally, there is a moment when the lights go out. It is not always possible, and is never easy, to distinguish the transition. The lights may be starting to grow dim when we imagine they are still shining brightly.

Such a period of transition came in Judah's history. Jeremiah was inactive during the latter part of Josiah's reign, but with the accession of Jehoiakim to the throne, the prophet began once more to be a spokesman for God rather than a spectator complacently viewing the superficial spirituality of Judah. A few historial facts must be brought before us in order to help us understand correctly and evaluate properly the ministry of Jeremiah during Jehoiakim's reign.

From 608 to 605 B.C. the Egyptian king, Pharaoh Necho, was the actual ruler of Judah. This was the same Necho against whom Josiah had been fighting when he was killed. The people of Judah placed Jehoahaz on the throne, but

Necho immediately summoned the new king to Hamath, placed him in chains, raised Eliakim to the throne, and changed his name to Jehoiakim. Necho's choice of this king was undoubtedly because he was in every way the opposite of his father Josiah. Almost immediately the religious situation was reversed, and the sins of Manasseh's day appeared again. Jehoiakim had no sympathy with the moral and spiritual claims of Jehovah as voiced by the prophetic party. It was inevitable that Jeremiah and Jehoiakim would clash. The king was self-centered and ungodly, with a mind closed to anything but his own wicked will. The prophet was humble in spirit, but his conviction was as deep as life itself, and he was unyielding in his determination to stand for righteousness.

The reign of Jehoiakim (608–597) is divided into two distinct periods. The point of division is the Battle of Carchemish (605), the battle which shifted the balance of power of world domination. Babylon defeated Assyria and took over the position of Judah's most powerful adversary. After the Battle of Carchemish the Assyrian empire was never considered again as a threat to Judah. It was Babylon who was to be the new "foe from the north."

There are fifteen passages from the book of Jeremiah which should be dated during the reign of Jehoiakim, five of them before the Battle of Carchemish. Three others were delivered sometime during Jehoiakim's reign, but it is not possible to determine whether they should be dated before or after the great battle.

There are three factors that assist in reaching a decision concerning the date. First, before 605 the prophet seemed to hold out some hope for Judah's deliverance, but after Carchemish the nation's fate seemed sealed. Jeremiah spoke as though she were unconditionally doomed beyond the point of redemption. Second, before Carchemish Jeremiah seemed vague about the actual country which would be the instrument of Jehovah in judgment. But after Babylon became the world master, Jeremiah no longer generalized. He became specific and named the country. Third, in 604, one year after Carchemish, Jeremiah was forced to flee for safety as a result of his clash with Jehoiakim over the burning of the roll (36:27-32). This meant that the prophet was no longer able to appear in public. Thus the symbolic messages of Jeremiah were probably delivered while the prophet was still permitted to move about freely. There were three sermons in symbol: "The Linen Girdle and the Shattered Jar" (13:1-17), "The Sermon from the Broken Bottle" (19:1 to 20:18), and "The Parable of the Potter" (18:1-23). These messages picture the prophet pleading for repentance while the lights of spiritual opportunity are still burning.

The Peril of Pride (13:1-17)

The material found in chapter 13 is, in reality, three independent addresses which were compiled because all of them deal with the same subject—the pride of Judah and the peril produced by such pride. Two of these addresses (vv. 1-11 and 12-17) concern the early years of Jehoiakim's reign. Jeremiah was commanded by the Lord to dramatize for the people their moral dilemma. At the word of Jehovah, Jeremiah bought a girdle. First, he put it on his body; then he went to the Euphrates River and hid it there in a cleft of the rock. After many days the prophet returned to the place and dug to find the girdle that he had buried. It was marred. Jehovah said, "After this manner will I mar the pride of Judah, and the great pride of Jerusalem. This evil people, that refuse to hear my words, that walk in the stubbornness of their heart . . . shall even be as this girdle, which is profitable for nothing" (13:9–10).

The prophet was then told to illustrate this truth again with the aid of jars. The containers were to be filled with wine and dashed against each other. In the same way Jehovah would dash against each other those who were haughty in spirit. There can be no doubt that these two messages were delivered during the period of national pride which was so characteristic of Jehoiakim's early years, before the Battle of Carchemish.

Pride is always the first step downward in the life of a nation or an individual. It was only a few hours before Peter denied his Lord that he boasted, "If all shall be offended in thee, I will never be offended" (Mat. 26:33). One of the Psalms speaks of pride "as a chain about their neck" (73:6), and another says, "The wicked, in the pride of his countenance, saith . . . There is no God" (10:4). The writer of Proverbs said, "Pride goeth before destruction, and a haughty spirit before a fall" (16:18). Isaiah spoke of the drunkards of Ephraim as the "crown of pride" (28:3). Ezekiel said that the iniquity of Sodom was "pride, fulness of bread, and prosperous ease" (16:49). He mentions further the pride of Egypt's power which shall surely come down (30:6). Daniel reported that when Nebuchadnezzar's "heart was lifted up, and his spirit was hardened so that he dealt proudly, he was deposed from his kingly throne, and they took his glory from him" (5:20). The prophet warned Nebuchadnezzar to "honor the King of heaven; for all his works are truth . . . and those that walk in pride he is able to abase" (Dan. 4:37). According to Hosea, the pride of Israel was a constant testimony of her spiritual poverty (5:5), and Obadiah told

Edom, "The pride of thy heart hath deceived thee. . . . Though thou mount on high as the eagle, and though thy nest be set among the stars, I will bring thee down from thence, saith Jehovah" (vv. 3–4). Zephaniah pictured the fruit of pride as breeding "nettles, and saltpits, and a perpetual desolation" (2:9). Zechariah warned that God would "cut off the pride of the Philistines"; "the pride of Assyria shall be brought down"; and the pride of the Jordan should be laid waste (9:6; 10:11; 11:3). Paul warned Timothy that a novice, if he is lifted up with pride, may fall into condemnation of the devil (1 Tim. 3:6).

With this abundant heritage of Scriptural warnings, is it any wonder that Lowell would call pride and weakness Siamese twins or that Louis XI would say, "When pride and presumption walk before, shame and loss follow very closely"? Benjamin Franklin gave a graphic picture as pride "breakfasted with plenty, dined with poverty and supped with infamy." Jeremiah was saying to Jehoiakim what William Knox searchingly inquired of the people of his day,

> Oh, why should the spirit of mortal be proud?
> Like a swift-flitting meteor, a fast-flying cloud,
> A flash of the lightning, a break of the wave,
> He passeth from life to his rest in the grave.

The Prophet and Punishment (19:1 to 20:18)

The two other symbolic messages of Jeremiah are related in that each has a connection with the potter and his work. Any consideration of chapters 19 and 20 must recognize that they are bound inseparably and should be studied as a unit. It is difficult at first to decide whether this section should be considered as coming before or after the Battle of

Carchemish. The evidence is strongest, however, for placing it in the early part of Jehoiakim's reign.

There are, in reality, three divisions within this section. First, in 19:1–15 Jeremiah was preaching another symbolic sermon. He took a bottle in his hand and led some of the political and religious leaders of Judah to the Valley of Hinnom. He then proclaimed fiery condemnation concerning the sins of the people. While the words were still fresh upon their ears, he broke the bottle in their presence and declared that Jehovah would break this people and this city in the same way. Jeremiah then returned to the court of the Temple and reaffirmed the message in the house of God.

The second division, 20:1–6, tells of the effect of the message and of Jeremiah's punishment because of the words he delivered for the Lord. Jeremiah was placed in stocks by Pashhur, the son of Immer the priest. The next day he was taken out of the stocks, whereupon he continued his warnings to Judah and particularly to Pashhur. The prophet went further in this message than he had ever gone. He named Babylon as the instrument of Jehovah's punitive hand. This may indicate that the Battle of Carchemish was near.

The remainder of the larger section, 20:7–18, consists of the prophet's lament. It was not spoken in public but was one of his private messages called by scholars "The Confessions of Jeremiah." These confessions are scattered throughout the entire roll of Jeremiah. Most of them were uttered throughout the reign of Jehoiakim during periods of despondency and gloom. They reveal much concerning the inner life of the prophet. Although Jeremiah was a prophet of God with a "thus saith the Lord," he was a human being with all the limitations of the flesh.

In this particular passage Jeremiah was lamenting because

he was an object of ridicule. "I am become a laughing-stock all the day, every one mocketh me. For as often as I speak, I cry out; I cry, Violence and destruction! because the word of Jehovah is made a reproach unto me, and a derision, all the day" (20:7–8). It is never popular to declare God's will to a crooked and perverse generation. It was not easy for Elijah to tell Ahab, "I have not troubled Israel; but thou, and thy father's house, in that ye have forsaken the commandments of Jehovah" (1 Kings 18:18). It was not easy for Nathan to tell David, "Thou art the man" (2 Sam. 12:7) nor for Micaiah to say, when all the other prophets had predicted success for Jehoshaphat, "I saw all Israel scattered upon the mountains, as sheep that have no shepherd" (1 Kings 22:17). But Jeremiah had the marks of a true prophet of God. He wrote out his resignation a number of times, although he never delivered it. There was always within him that which constrained him to preach: "And if I say, I will not make mention of him, nor speak any more in his name, then there is in my heart as it were a burning fire shut up in my bones, and I am weary with forbearing, and I cannot contain" (20:9). For the man who truly understands it, the call of God is stronger than the call of men.

Why this taunting of the people? The first impression would be that the jeers were because Jeremiah dared to suggest that a foreign invader could conquer Judah. A closer examination, however, reveals that it was rather because Jeremiah named the country. It was Babylon who was to be God's instrument of punishment. Jeremiah was saying that not through the decaying Assyrian empire but through the rising star of Babylon would the century-old prophecy of Isaiah made during the days of Hezekiah (Isa. 39:6–7) be fulfilled.

79

The Prophet and the Potter (18:1-23)

This is the most familiar of the symbolic messages of Jeremiah. At this point we are dealing particularly with the eighteenth chapter, but we must remember that chapters 18-20 form one basic unit concerning the potter and his work and the political fate of Judah. There is good reason to believe that these three chapters existed as a separate roll and circulated independently before being incorporated into the general roll of Jeremiah. Although we are treating chapter 18 after chapters 19-20, it should be pointed out that evidence indicates that this chapter should be dated slightly earlier than the other two. There seems to be some possibility that Judah might amend her ways and submit herself to God's will.

Most scholars see this event as one of the most decisive in the career of the prophet. Kirkpatrick finds in the story of the potter the fundamental passage in the Old Testament with reference to the conditional element in prophecy. Nowhere else is this set forth more clearly. Skinner sees this as the classic illustration of divine sovereignty and believes that this conception of the potter and clay is original with Jeremiah. George Adam Smith sees in this section a divine as well as a human free will. God is not fettered by his previous decrees. He deals with men on a moral basis. He treats them as their moral conduct permits him to do.

This event occurred during the early part of Jehoiakim's reign. The king had reversed all of the policies of his predecessor. Even though Josiah's policies had degenerated into patriotic zeal rather than religious devotion, Judah's moral condition was much improved under his reign. For all his faults, Josiah was one of the godliest kings who ever sat upon the throne of Judah. But Josiah was dead and Jehoiakim was ruler in Judah. Jeremiah was no longer a popular prophet. He had become a prophet without a patron. He felt like Elijah under the juniper tree or John the Baptist in prison at Macherus. Was God still sovereign, or had evil forced him to abdicate? If he were righteous, why had he allowed Jehoiakim to gain control of the land? Every person of God has his periods of skepticism, and this was Jeremiah's day to doubt. In the midst of this questioning God sent him to the house of the potter. Just as Newton had probably seen many apples falling before that great day of the revelation, so many times before the prophet had seen the potter, with his lump of clay and pan of water, sitting at his frame turning the wheel with his foot. This time, however, the message was vibrant and vital. The clay was marred, but the potter did not discard it. He fashioned it into another vessel. For the first time Jeremiah saw a truth that had been unrecognized before his eyes. Judah was a marred vessel, but the Potter could reshape it into a fit instrument for divine use.

It seems that Kirkpatrick's observation is one of the most relevant. Much has been said about Old Testament prophecy. There are two extreme schools of thought concerning this important part of Old Testament literature. One is that history is prewritten in many of the prophetic messages of such men as Isaiah, Jeremiah, and Ezekiel. Literal details are emphasized, and it is held that the prophet foresaw with amazing and uncanny accuracy detailed events thousands of years before they came to pass. The other extreme is contending, as some scholars do, that the prophet spoke only in general principles and that predictive prophecy is nonexistent or at least a bare minimum in the Old Testament. There is not, however, an either/or choice. Certainly anyone who has made a study of Old Testament prophecy has seen that the prophet was more than a mere predictor of future events without a message relevant for his own day.

A consecrated Christian can believe in the integrity of the Scriptures and maintain that the prophets were as much "forth-tellers" as "fore-tellers." This is not to deny predictive prophecy. There are examples of predictive prophecy in the Old Testament that are amazing. God saw fit to breathe into the prophets an ability to foresee great events and tell his people about them. But the prophet was also a "forth-teller." He spoke a message which was relevant to the moral and spiritual need of the day. Some people find it fascinating to deal with symbols and signs and attempt to find clues to future events in history by this method. The greater message of prophecy, however, is that these men of God spoke moral and spiritual truth which is applicable to every generation. It should mean much more to a Christian to see in the messages of Ezekiel and Daniel that God's purposes will be successful in history than to multiply a few figures together and try to predict the date of the next war.

This passage concerning the potter shows that God deals with his people upon the basis of their moral choices. God is the unconditional ally of no people. It is only those who work righteousness who are accepted with him. Failure to see this basic truth was Israel's folly throughout all the prophetic period. It was the task of the prophets to warn their generation that God could and would make even the land of Israel "an astonishment, and a perpetual hissing; every one that passeth thereby shall be astonished, and shake his head" (18:16). The people, though they were a chosen people, could be scattered "as with an east wind before the enemy," and God could and would show even Judah "the back, and not the face, in the day of their calamity" (18:17).

The Lord has always dealt with his people on the conditional principle. In the early years of Israel's history, as a group of liberated slaves stood within the shadow of Sinai, God laid before them this challenge and promise, "Ye have seen what I did unto the Egyptians, and how I bare you on eagles' wings, and brought you unto myself. Now therefore, if ye will obey my voice indeed, and keep my covenant, then ye shall be mine own possession from among all peoples . . . and ye shall be unto me a kingdom of priests, and a holy nation" (Ex. 19:4–6).

These symbolic messages, especially the one of the potter and the wheel, show that Judah's lights were still burning. If she would but know the things which belong to her peace, the house would not become desolate. Judah must recognize that even as the snows of Lebanon must not fail and the cold waters that flow down from afar must not be dried up, so the righteousness of Judah must not give way to the burning of incense to false gods (18:14–15). Judah must repent lest the people continue "to stumble in their ways, in the ancient paths, to walk in bypaths, in a way not cast up" (18:15). The people must turn from their own devices and each one from after the stubbornness of his evil heart.

In the eighteenth century England and France faced a similar situation. A few years before the outbreak of the French Revolution and the resulting Reign of Terror a man of God with conviction and courage preached a sermon in the court of Louis XVI. The message was soul stirring. He told of the spiritual need in France and pleaded with the reigning monarch to act in an effort to end the oppression, selfishness, and perversion of justice. King Louis, however, was one of the few present who had enjoyed a full meal. He went to sleep, and the rest of the sermon was accompanied by royal snores which were audible to the entire court. How different might have been the history of France if her leaders had listened while the lights were still burning.

Across the English Channel the eighteenth century was a critical period for England also. An ambassador to England reported to his country that Christianity in England was a thing of the past. Vitality was gone from the religious life of the people, and there was a dearth of spiritual power in the churches. The clergy was becoming more worldly, and the "like people, like priests" of Hosea's preaching was reflected in low standards of the people in personal conduct and everyday living. Sir William Blackstone made the statement that he had attended every church in London and "heard not one discourse which had more Christianity in it than the writings of Cicero." Green, in his *Short History of the English People*, declares, "The English clergy were the idlest and most lifeless in the world." E. N. Hardy says that "church attendance had gradually dwindled till many absented themselves from practically all services save those of a festive occasion, yet formalism everywhere prevailed and a certain respect for the church existed." The form was there, but the churches had lost life and power.

But man's extremity is always God's opportunity, and he always works through human instruments. Three men and their associates changed the history of England. George Whitefield and the Wesleys, led by the Spirit of God, saved England from a "reign of terror."

Jeremiah was confident that Judah could be spared. The lights were still burning, and the Potter had a purpose. The nation need only amend its ways.

7

"The Dear Lord's Best Interpreters"

One of the saddest sights to be found on the contemporary scene—or in any period of history—is the decadence of a strong family. Here, for instance, is a family that at one time possessed vitality and strength. It was a leading power, a pillar of strength and influence in the community. From generation to generation, however, the strain weakened, and a century later the grandchildren are virtually dependent upon society.

This story has been repeated in almost every area of activity. A strong personality emerges from obscurity, perhaps from the other side of the tracks. He is a driver, an administrator, an empire builder. He singlehandedly builds a great business within a generation. At the peak of financial success and business expansion he must give up the reins. His children carry on but not nearly so well. They enjoy the luxury created by their father. They think "dear old Dad" worked too hard, which accounted for his premature death. He should have spent more time with his family, for if he had not pushed himself so unceasingly, he might still be living today. He was one of the old school which in our day is disappearing from off the scene. His children have no compunction of conscience, however, about spending the money on their personal desires, even though it was earned by "old school" methods. By the third generation there is not enough business judgment in the family to earn a decent living. Somebody out in the sticks or across the tracks will have to do it again.

The same principle operates in political life. Nations have existed several generations beyond their time because some great statesman stamped the imprint of his personality upon the annals of his country and the life of his people.

In no realm is this law more evident than in the moral and spiritual areas of family life. A great, godly family plows deep religious furrows. Convictions as deep as life itself are embedded in the hearts of the children. With a little modern education, however, the sons and daughters decide a more tolerant approach is desirable. The tolerance gives way to apathy, and by the time a third generation comes, the spiritual life of that family can best be described thus: "The first generation believed the creed, the second generation doubted it, and the third generation has never read it."

Great churches and religious institutions follow this cycle. A spiritual giant appears on the scene. As a result of his leadership a church or Christian institution comes into being. For many years the name of this godly man is associated with the life of this organization. Another generation comes along, and the founder is treated with token respect. "He was a fine man for his day, but our approach is different." By the next generation he is an antiquated individual of an outdated era. There are, of course, exceptions to these illustrations, but there is much truth in the description of these patterns and processes.

It is against this background of thought that we should approach the thirty-fifth chapter of Jeremiah. The story of the Rechabites gives a picture of a family with religious convictions that had lasted four generations. They serve as an example of a family strain that did not die. This section (35:1-17) stands as a part of the book which is separate from the context in that it could be eliminated from the text without in any way destroying the continuity of the prophetic ministry of Jeremiah.

The most logical date for the chapter is during the latter part of Jehoiakim's reign, after the Battle of Carchemish. Some scholars have placed the event very soon after the great battle and have maintained that the eleventh verse does not necessarily mean Nebuchadnezzar came in person upon these raiding expeditions. Rather, his armies invaded the land. This seems to be within the realm of probability and would no doubt satisfy the meaning of the verse. Other students of Jeremiah think, however, that this event occurred at the close of Jehoiakim's reign, perhaps even during the three months of Jehoiachin's. The actual date we shall probably never know, nor is it important. The important truth here is the spiritual lesson to be received from the Rechabites.

Religious Reactionaries

The Rechabites were the watchdogs of orthodoxy. They represented that group in Judah which had rigidly refused to amalgamate socially or religiously, even to the slightest degree, with the Canaanites of the land. In order to understand these people it is necessary to go back to the days of Moses and Joshua. During the 430 years that Israel was in Egypt the land of Canaan was completely saturated with the religion of the pagan tribes that inhabited the land. Their worship has been discussed in a number of books, one of the best being Leslie's *Old Testament Religion*. As the worshipers engaged in the immoral and licentious ceremonies of the cults, they were attempting to gain the favor of the local gods of the soil and thus assure the fertility of the land. The ever-present threat to Israel was that her pure monotheistic devotion to Jehovah would be contaminated by the Canaanitish worship. This is the background for the Second Commandment in the Decalogue; it is also, to a large extent, the reason for the harsh treatment of the enemies of Israel throughout the period from Joshua to David. Such perverted religion, immoral and incestuous, could not be evangelized. It must, like a cancerous growth, be removed lest it mutilate Judah's spiritual life with its own deadly malignancy.

As Israel became a settled people, her religion took on an urbanized color. This does not mean the entire nation became followers of the Canaanitish form of worship (although in some periods of her history the apostasy seemed to have been virtually universal), but it does mean that at least socially the nomadic influence gave way to customs such as would be adopted by city dwellers. The strict code and customs of rural life gave way to a more impersonalized way of living in the city. It was at this point that the Rechabites took their stand. They resolutely refused to become city dwellers. To them the city symbolized sin, and to plant a crop or build a house for a permanent dwelling was a step in the direction of that which would be fatal to their spiritual life.

If this attitude seems somewhat amusing to people of the twentieth century, to them it was a serious matter. The truth is that if these Rechabites and their counterparts have gone too far in one direction, much contemporary religious thinking has gone too far in the other. We need these Rechabites today to stabilize society. It is very popular and some writers think it very clever to speak with smug complacency of Victorian England or Puritan New England or a strait-laced Southern Bible belt, but these periods and these people contributed more to moral standards and godly environment than all the modern schools of theology have been able to construct with the products of their thinking. Some of these spiritual giants of yesteryear may not have talked so much about social consciousness, but their communities were centers of holy living and godly families. Someone once visited a small village in England and observed the unusual love for holy things and the absence of worldly pleasures. He asked for an explanation of this unusual attitude and was told that a century before, a man named John Wesley had preached there. The blind bard was regarded by some in his day as too conservative in religious convictions, but years later Wordsworth could say,

> Milton! thou shouldst be living at this hour;
> England hath need of thee; she is a fen
> Of stagnant waters . . . return to us again. . . .
> Thy soul was like a Star. . . .

Everyone who is a serious thinker realizes that a streamlined age such as ours needs Victorian virtues and Puritanic patterns and Rechabite religion more than it needs a further step in the modernizing of morals. The watchdog of orthodoxy is never popular, but he is a necessity in any day.

Family Fidelity

From these rural people comes another truth much needed in our generation. Loyalty is one of the most noble characteristics a man may possess. Jonadab, son of Rechab, had commanded his family, "Ye shall drink no wine, neither ye, nor your sons, for ever: neither shall ye build house, nor sow seed, nor plant vineyard, nor have any; but all your days ye shall dwell in tents; that ye may live many days in the land wherein ye sojourn" (35:6–7).

The point for emphasis at this moment is not the virtue of the vow but the fact that these Rechabites were faithful in their observance of the oath. This, in fact, is the pivotal teaching of the entire chapter. Jeremiah brought the Rechabites into the Temple, set before them bowls of wine, and invited them to drink of it. They refused, citing as their reason the ancient vow of their family. They immediately declared that the only reason they were inside the city now was for protection from the armies of Chaldea and Syria. Many Bible students think that the Rechabites had probably pitched their tents within the city walls and were thus still living in tents, not houses, even though they were inside the city.

Jeremiah was then directed by Jehovah to use the Rechabites as an object lesson for Judah. These tent dwellers would drink no wine because they were obedient to their father. Judah, too, had an obligation. Jehovah had guided her spiritual life during the years by means of prophetic truth, but Judah had shown less judgment in spiritual matters than these primitive people. This passage might be said to have its New Testament parallel in the words of Jesus concerning the centurion, "I have not found so great faith, no, not in Israel" (Matt. 8:10).

A constant source of chagrin today is that many times people who have more Christian light are found guilty of being less dedicated to the purposes of God than some who are not so privileged in spiritual matters. Jesus had more difficulty in his day with the people known as religious leaders than with any other group. The most severe pronouncements in the New Testament are those by Jesus in the twenty-third chapter of Matthew's Gospel. They were uttered to the people who occupied places of superiority in the Jewish religious organization.

The Christian world today needs families with the spiritual fidelity of these ancient sons of Jonadab. There are godly values which need conserving. Family life needs to be held intact. Strong family strains have always made great contributions to the life of a nation. There is no more convincing example of this than the family of Jonathan Edwards. A study of his descendants reveals that from this family have come two hundred and ninety-five college graduates, one hundred lawyers, one hundred or more ministers and missionaries, seventy-five army officers, sixty or more authors, sixty physicians, and thirteen college presidents.

The home and the family remain the basic unit of society. The Rechabites recognized that an urbanized way of life made it difficult for family life to be stable. The program of the average person in the city is not conducive to a well-ordered family life. Someone has described a modern young girl's attitude toward home thus: "What do I need with a home? I was born in a hospital, educated in a college, courted in an automobile. I live out of the delicatessen and paper bags. I spend my mornings at the bridge table, my afternoons on the golf course, and my evenings at the movies. When I die I will be buried in a cemetery. What do I need with a home? All I need is a garage."

Another factor which causes family life to be difficult in urbanized society is the informality of social life. The entertainment world has introduced a free and easygoing attitude toward marital partnerships, seemingly harmless swapping of affections, and the modern ballroom dance with its potential perils. The rural philosophy of life disapproves of these attitudes, and the Rechabites are right. These Rechabites are more than a group of queer fanatics from another century. They represent a principle of family life. Even in the midst of a highly urban society today we find families who maintain conservative patterns of living. They "live in tents" and "drink no wine" in the sense that they do not sell their birthright of family heritage and Christian morals for a mess of "urban pottage." They live in the midst of city worldliness, but they never become a part of it. God places some of his Rechabites in the city in order that they may carry his message and hold high his standard in the places where cross the crowded ways of life. Isaiah, Jeremiah, Spurgeon, Phillips Brooks, Henry Ward Beecher, and Dwight L. Moody were men who were sent to the city people with God's word. There is heartbreak for the man of God in a crowded city, but the homes of these great metropolitan areas need strong stakes. God loves all people, including those who live in the cities.

Divine Decree

The latter part of this chapter (vv. 16–17) gives the verdict of Jehovah concerning the people of Judah as well as the Rechabites. Because Judah had ignored the repeated warnings and pleadings of Jehovah's messengers, her fate was sealed. All the pronouncements of doom which had been uttered by the prophets upon Judah's failure to return to Jehovah would become a reality. They had refused to answer the divine call, and there was no alternative. The God of Israel must come in judgment. He must send evil upon the land. A righteous God cannot treat sin lightly. A covenant-breaking people must be punished.

What then of the Rechabites? God said through Jeremiah that the Rechabites would continue to stand before him. "Thus saith Jehovah of hosts, the God of Israel: Because ye have obeyed the commandment of Jonadab your father, and kept all his precepts . . . Jonadab the son of Rechab shall not want a man to stand before me for ever" (v. 18).

Was this promise literally fulfilled? How long was "for ever" in the mind of the prophet? There are scholars who believe Rechabites did not remain faithful and cite Nehemiah 3:14: "And the dung gate repaired Malchijah the son of Rechab, the ruler of the district of Beth-haccherem." This does not seem to be sufficient proof, however, to warrant such a sweeping conclusion. There are many examples of similar names. Even in the book of Jeremiah there are several other men with the same name as the prophet.

Another school of thought contends that some of the Rechabites were incorporated into subordinate ranks of the clergy, but this lacks sufficient evidence to be accepted as factual. It is true that the phrase "to stand before Jehovah" can mean "to minister to him," but this is not its only meaning. Moreover, if this rendering of the verb be taken as correct, it still does not necessarily prove that the Rechabites became priests. Some individuals may have become priests, as there is a record in one of the accounts of the martyrdom of James of "one of the priests of the sons of Rechab, the sons of Rechabim, who are mentioned by Jeremiah the prophet." Similarly, some individual Rechabites may have compromised and become city dwellers. The passage in Nehemiah may refer to these people. The truth is that we do not know. The Rechabites are lost in history.

What do we know, then, for certain? We know there has been a spiritual fulfilment of this declaration of Jeremiah. There have been in all generations men with the spiritual convictions and religious outlook of the Rechabites. These people have refused to blend in with the color of the times. They have been labeled as ultraconservative, and indeed they are. These people are not often persecuted or mistreated. They are merely ignored as modern society moves from one fad to another seeking the thrill of novelty. Yet these conservers of spiritual values continue to live simple godly lives. Some of them are in every community. They remain as exponents and examples of the simple life of our Saviour. Our society needs the stabilizing influence of the Rechabites.

8

"Better Had They Ne'er Been Born"

The thirty-sixth chapter of Jeremiah records the most strategic moment in the prophet's ministry. There are at least three reasons for considering the material in this chapter as part of the most important in the book. First, it is here that Jeremiah for the first time put his prophecies into written form. The book of Jeremiah is different from most of the Old Testament literature in that there is at least a partial record of the actual compilation of the book. Part of that compilation is recorded in this thirty-sixth chapter.

From a political standpoint this record is of superlative significance. The date of the material in 36:1–4 is the "fourth year of Jehoiakim," generally accepted as 605 B.C. This same year the Battle of Carchemish ended with Babylon the victorious master of the Near East. Judah then became a vassal of Babylon. The effect of this upon Jeremiah will be discussed later.

A final reason for considering this material as decisive is that the king's rejection of the prophetic warning was probably the act which sealed the fate of Judah. Until Jehoiakim's burning of the roll there was still hope for Judah and a chance for her deliverance, but afterward Jeremiah spoke as though the last flicker of Judah's opportunity had passed. There are three major divisions to this section.

Recorded (36:1–8)

The student of Jeremiah must always keep before him the importance of the Battle of Carchemish and its relation to Jehoiakim and the subsequent ministry of Jeremiah. A century before, Isaiah had warned Ahaz that Rezin of Syria and Pekah of Israel were but "two tails of smoking firebrands" (7:4) and had spoken of Judah's mutual security alliance with Egypt as a bed "shorter than that a man can stretch himself on it; and the covering narrower than that he can wrap himself in it" (28:20). Isaiah and Jeremiah were not only prophets of God with a spiritual message for the people, they were godly statesmen with divine directions for the leaders of the nation. Jerusalem was saved in 701 B.C. from the Assyrian army because at the last moment Hezekiah heeded the prophet of God.

Judah faced a similar situation. The field of international politics had changed a bit, but it was still the struggle for balance of power, and Judah was once again caught in the web of ambition and intrigue. She was always an ideal nation to be used as a buffer state for a would-be conqueror. Assyria had moved off the scene. Babylon had replaced her as the world master, but Egypt was still a strong enough factor that Babylon wanted Judah for the protection she could give as a buffer state. In the days of Isaiah there had existed a strong pro-Egyptian party in Judah, and fragments of this school of thought still remained. The important historical fact in the consideration of this chapter is that it was Babylon who was the dominant power.

What did the outcome of the Battle of Carchemish mean to Jeremiah? He had begun his ministry by preaching that judgment was coming from the north. The youthful preacher uttered his warning with great alarm as though the invader were knocking at the door. The truth is, however, that the foe from the north did not materialize. The Scythians, if these were the people whom Jeremiah had in mind, did not overrun the land. They bypassed Judah, raided the coastal cities, and descended into Egypt. Were Jeremiah's stirring warnings thus useless? Did the great reformation of 621 serve to alter God's punitive hand? Was Jeremiah discredited as a prophet for a season when the northern foe failed to come? Perhaps the expression "foe from the north" became a phrase of jest and was used as a taunting refrain by the people when the prophet began, in the early years of Jehoiakim, to speak once more about judgment. There is one thing, however, that is certain. When Babylon became master of the world, Jeremiah once more began to see a "boiling caldron, with its face from the north." It was while he was in this frame of mind that God spoke to the prophet.

As far as is known, Jeremiah up to this time had not recorded any of his messages. It is, of course, to be expected that he had made notes for his own personal use, but there existed no roll containing his oracles or sermons. There are references on at least two occasions of "a book" and at least one letter containing his messages (25:13; 29:1; 30:2).

The prophet's mind now began to clear. He saw more than "men as trees walking" (Mark 8:24). He saw rather the entire truth concerning the foe from the north. God was going to use Babylon as the agent of chastisement for his people. Babylon would be to Judah and Jerusalem what Assyria had been to Israel and Samaria. There was only one chance. Jeremiah would put all his prophecies in writing and present them to the people. Perhaps they would heed the prophet of God. Jeremiah called Baruch and dictated these messages to him. He then commanded Baruch to go to the Temple and read these messages on a fast day to the people. Jeremiah gave as his reason for not going himself: "I am shut up; I cannot go into the house of Jehovah" (36:5). This does not mean that he was in prison and probably does not speak of his being ceremonially unclean. The best interpretation is that Jeremiah's being excluded from the Temple is to be connected with the clash between Jeremiah and Pashhur (20:1–6).

Jeremiah was a true prophet of God. His recording of the roll represents an all-out effort to turn Judah back from her mad race to certain death. Perhaps the cumulative effect of his entire ministry in written form might serve to bring the people to repentance where the individual and isolated messages had failed.

Mention should be made at this point of one other section which is related to the dictating of these prophecies. Chapter 45, which consists of only six verses, should be studied after verse 8 of chapter 36. That short chapter records the words of Jehovah through Jeremiah to Baruch when the latter became despondent. Jeremiah's condemnation of Judah's sin and his warning of impending judgment had added sorrow to Baruch's pain and made him weary with groaning. Baruch was told he was not to seek great things for himself. The land would be invaded, all which had been built up would be broken down, but Baruch's life would be spared.

Most students of Jeremiah think Baruch wrote these words as he looked back upon the scene some years later. Perhaps as the rolls of prophecies and biography of Jeremiah were

98

compiled by Baruch he placed this small bit about himself last because of timidity or modesty. There is good reason to believe that in one stage of the development of the book these six verses represented the concluding chapter. Later the roll of foreign prophecies (chs. 46–51) and the historical appendix covering the fall of Jerusalem (ch. 52) were added.

It should be pointed out, however, that in reality Baruch did receive great things for himself. The privilege of being Jeremiah's personal amanuensis has brought him a fame through the centuries that could never have been equalled by any amount of personal comfort or security in the latter days of his own lifetime. As long as the world speaks of Jeremiah, they will also remember the one man who meant so much to him, Baruch, the son of Neriah.

Read and Rejected (36:9–26)

The prophet's words were not immediately read to the people. According to verses 9 and 10, it was the ninth month of the next year when Baruch read the roll in the Temple in the chamber of Gemariah, the son of Shaphan the scribe. Some have endeavored to explain this long delay by calling attention to the difference between the Hebrew and Babylonian calendars. Skinner points out that the Hebrew years were reckoned according to the Hebrew calendar from harvest to harvest, while the numbering of the months followed the Babylonian calendar whose year began in the spring. If this view were adopted and applied here, there would be a lapse of only about three months between the dictating and the reading of the roll. Skinner's theory is attractive, but it is probably safer to stay with the most obvious interpretation and assume that at least nine months passed before the roll was read.

The question is immediately asked, "Why should Baruch wait so long before delivering Jeremiah's message?" There are two possible reasons. First, perhaps the Battle of Carchemish had not actually been fought when Jeremiah dictated the roll. It could be that Jeremiah perceived the outcome of the battle. Jehovah might have revealed to him that Babylon would be victorious and told him to prepare the roll. He was not to make the roll public, however, until the battle was over and the people had received news of its outcome. It would require almost a year for them to absorb all the implications of Babylon's victory and feel the full force of the crisis.

The other possible reason is that the prophet and Baruch were waiting for a day when the largest possible number of people would be present in the Temple to hear the message. The ninth verse tells that the people proclaimed a fast. This indicates that the people were more concerned about the situation than the king was. Leslie suggests that the fast was related to the lack of rain, but this is extremely doubtful. It was the concern and even alarm of the people for the safety of their homes and country. Even the Rechabites had already come, or would be shortly coming, to the city, which was for them an unheard-of thing. Already the new northern foe was on its way. Jeremiah and Baruch may have delayed a number of months, but they chose a most opportune time. Surely Judah would hear!

Important to a consideration of this roll is the question of its contents. It is true that the text represents Jehovah as saying, "Write . . . all the words that I have spoken unto thee against Israel, and against Judah, and against all the nations, from the day I spake unto thee, from the days of Josiah, even unto this day" (36:2). A strictly literal interpretation of this passage would mean that if it were known which messages in the present book of Jeremiah were delivered before the fourth year of Jehoiakim, it could be stated with finality that they were the ones contained in the original roll. But the matter is not that simple. For one thing, Old Testament students are too familiar with this Hebrew word for "all" to build any dogmatic case of literal interpretation upon it. It could be that Jeremiah prepared a roll which contained the totality of his message without including every word of every discourse. The roll was read at least three times in one day, and the inference is that it was read completely without interruption each time. The Bible record does not, of course, comment either way upon its length, but there is nothing to indicate that it was of unusual length. The twenty-third verse speaks of three or four leaves, but the better translation is "three or four columns." In fact, the reading of the roll indicates a summary of the prophetic messages rather than a detailed reproduction of a number of manuscripts.

Another factor which makes it difficult to determine the contents of the original roll is that the prophet was later commanded, "Take thee again another roll, and write in it all the former words that were in the first roll, which Jehoiakim the king of Judah hath burned" (36:28). The last verse of the chapter states that Baruch wrote at the dictation of Jeremiah "all the words of the book which Jehoiakim king of Judah had burned in the fire." It also adds, however, that "there were added besides unto them many like words" (v. 32). If this latter statement be taken into consideration, it would seem that it is an impossible task to ascertain the exact contents of either roll. Were additions made to each individual message, or were new messages added, or both? If the writer were called upon for a personal judgment, it would be that the major part of the first roll would be found in chapters 1–6;

101

7:1 to 8:3; 18:1–23; 19:1 to 20:18; 22:1–9, 13–23; 25:1–38; 13:1–17, and also some, perhaps most or all, of the foreign prophecies. There are a number of threats of punishments in these sections, and these would account for the alarm among the people and princes who heard Baruch read the roll.

A solemn day had come for Judah. The situation was so serious that a fast had been declared. The people were contemplating the peril which might be facing them. Would God protect them if an enemy should attempt to invade the city? Already word had come that Babylon was marching toward Judah. Baruch chose this as the time to read the words of Jeremiah. He went to the chamber of Gemariah, which was near one of the gates of the Temple. At this time Gemariah had left his son Micaiah in charge of affairs. As Baruch read, a silence fell over the people. The words told of Judah's sin and of Jehovah's repeated attempts to woo them back to righteousness. When Baruch closed with the declaration that the nation must repent or face the full force of God's fury, there was a silence.

Micaiah realized, as did all the people, that these statements were too factual to be ignored. He dashed to the king's house and went into the chamber of Elishama, the scribe. Here Micaiah's father, Gemariah, and all of the princes were gathered together. It is not inconceivable that they were discussing the possibility of Nebuchadnezzar's following up his victory at Carchemish with an all-out effort to invade Judah and let its people know immediately that Judah was the vassal of Babylon. Micaiah rushed in and breathlessly declared what he had heard, quoting from memory the substance of as many phrases as he could recall. The already concerned princes sent Jehudi to bring Baruch to their chamber. At the word of the princes, Baruch read the roll to them.

Looking at one another with fear and anxiety, they interrogated Baruch concerning the source of the roll. They resolved to tell the king immediately, but they first warned Baruch, "Go, hide thee, thou and Jeremiah; and let no man know where ye are" (36:19).

The princes lost no time in going directly to Jehoiakim the king. For some reason, however, they did not take Baruch's roll with them. Perhaps in their haste they forgot the roll, or more likely, it may be that they hoped he would accept their oral report. Jehoiakim's first response, however, was to send Jehudi to bring the roll. Jehudi then began to read the contents in the hearing of Jehoiakim and the others. The king was sitting near the fire. As Jehudi read three or four columns, the king took his penknife, cut them off, and cast them into the fire. As Jehudi read more, the king cut and tossed them into the fire until the entire roll was consumed. Neither the king nor his servants showed any concern nor evidenced any consideration for the roll or his princes. Several times some of the princes endeavored in vain to dissuade the king from destroying the roll. As he finished, he turned to his son and several of his servants and commanded them to arrest Jeremiah and Baruch.

The Scripture does not indicate a great rage on Jehoiakim's part as he burned the roll, but a cold and icy defiance to the prophet's message. That he burned the roll section by section rather than all at once indicates a deliberate defiance of, and complete contempt for, the word of Jehovah.

Rewritten (36:27–32)

But God is not so easily declared irrelevant to the life of an individual or a nation. Napoleon said there was no God, but God said there shall be no Napoleon. And God always has the last word. One historian said, "The Duke of Wellington did not win the Battle of Waterloo. Who won it? God won it. Napoleon bothered the Almighty." In the New Testament Jesus told a group of people who were in the process of rejecting the eternal Word of God, "Therefore I say unto you, The kingdom of God shall be taken away from you, and shall be given to a nation bringing forth the fruits thereof. And he that falleth on this stone shall be broken to pieces: but on whomsoever it shall fall, it will scatter him as dust" (Matt. 21:43–44).

"The word of Jehovah came unto Jonah the second time" (Jonah 3:1). It always reappears—sometimes in renewed invitation and sometimes in declared condemnation. In the case of Jeremiah and Jehoiakim, it was the latter. The prophet was told to write in another roll the same messages that were in the roll burned by Jehoiakim. Jehovah then added an additional note concerning the king: "Therefore thus saith Jehovah concerning Jehoiakim king of Judah: He shall have none to sit upon the throne of David; and his dead body shall be cast out in the day to the heat, and in the night to the frost. And I will punish him and his seed and his servants for their iniquity; and I will bring upon them, and upon the inhabitants of Jerusalem, and upon the men of Judah, all the evil that I have pronounced against them" (36:30–31).

There have, of course, been two objections to the pronouncement of Jeremiah. First, it has been pointed out the statement that Jehoiakim "shall have none to sit upon the throne of David" was not literally fulfilled. Jehoiachin, his son, ruled for three months and ten days. This is another of the many examples of the difficulty of expecting a literal fulfilment of a spiritual truth. Jeremiah's prophecy was certainly fulfilled in spirit inasmuch as Jehoiachin reigned only a brief period and was taken captive to Babylon, where he remained a prisoner for thirty-seven years. For those, however, who insist upon a literal fulfilment of every prophecy there is some comfort in a strictly literal translation of the Hebrew: "Therefore thus saith Jehovah concerning Jehoiakim, king of Judah: There shall not be to him one sitting upon the throne of David." The phrase "shall not be" is an imperfect, and the force of the imperfect is usually continuous action. This would mean that the seed of Jehoiakim would not be able to sit continuously, or remain, on the throne of Judah. A similar interpretation is found in 1 John 3:9: "Whosoever is born of God doth not go on sinning [as a life policy] because his seed remaineth in him and he cannot go on practicing sin."

This approach seems to reveal exactly the message and meaning of the prophet. The seed of Jehoiakim would not occupy a permanent place upon the throne of David. Jeremiah's prophecy was, in this sense, literally fulfilled. The three months and ten days of Jehoiachin's reign would have no inclination of permanency. The next king was Zedekiah, another son of Josiah. After his reign the kingdom of Judah ceased to exist, and the nation went into captivity. Judah was never ruled again by a king. Upon the return from Babylonian captivity she was guided politically as well as spiritually by her priests, scribes, and religious leaders.

There is another objection which has been brought against this prophecy of Jeremiah. The prophet described the treatment which Jehoiakim's body would receive by saying, "His dead body shall be cast out in the day to the heat, and in the night to the frost" (36:30). These words should be compared with a similar thought concerning Jehoiakim which was undoubtedly written at the same time: "He shall be buried with the burial of an ass, drawn and cast forth beyond the gates of Jerusalem" (22:19). These latter words are a part of a prophecy concerning Jehoiakim found in an independent roll (22:1 to 23:40) of Jeremiah's messages. The roll contains a series of prophecies concerning the kings of Judah (22:1 to 23:8) and the false prophets (23:9–40).

The question of whether Jehoiakim's death and burial were in accordance with the words of the prophet also arises. The author of Chronicles states nothing of his death or burial, and the author of 2 Kings states only that he "slept with his fathers" (24:6). The significant point is that neither of the historians give us any details of his burial. This is a strong indication that there was something unusual about his burial when we recall that, with the exception of Hezekiah, we have a record of the burial of every king of Judah except Jehoiakim. Skinner reaches this conclusion:

Two possibilities remain open: the death of this unpopular monarch may have been followed by a tumult in which his dead body was dishonoured by the mob. Or the Chaldeans, when they entered the city, may have disinterred the corpse and exposed it to the indignities here described. . . . Some kind of fulfilment the prophecy must have had, or its substance would hardly have been preserved in two separate forms.[1]

This section might well be closed with four practical observations: First, one does not alter a fact by ignoring it. Alexander Maclaren says, "It is not pre-eminent seamanship to put the look-out man in irons because he sings out, 'Breakers ahead.' The crew does not abolish the reef so, but they end their last chance of avoiding it, and presently the shock comes and the cruel coral tears through the hull."

Second, the reason one rejects the written word is because

he has already rejected the living Word. Behind the New Testament is the Word made flesh. Men are not saved by the written word but by the living Word of God. Mary A. Lathbury wrote,

> Beyond the sacred page
> I seek Thee, Lord;
> My spirit pants for Thee,
> O living Word.

The written Word is a vehicle to bring men to Christ, the living Word. Jehoiakim rejected the roll of Jeremiah because he had already rejected the God of Jeremiah.

Third, one does not break God's laws. He only breaks himself on those laws. Jehoiakim's death is a demonstration that the mill of God's punitive hand grinds exceeding small. The anvil will remain unharmed long after the hammers are worn with beating years of time. Those who reject the revealed will of God may find their life summarized in the words of the fisherman, "We toiled all night, and took nothing" (Luke 5:5). Perhaps Scott's words apply as aptly to Jehoiakim as to anyone:

> Better had they ne'er been born
> That read to doubt or read to scorn.

Fourth, only in God's will is our peace. The grass shall wither and the flower of the field shall fade, but the word of God shall endure because it is a record of his will.

9

"New Occasions Teach New Duties"

The third and final chapter in the life and ministry of Jeremiah may be said to begin with the accession of Zedekiah to the throne of Judah. In reality, however, the death of Jehoiakim draws the curtain on act two, and there is a parenthetical period between his death and the beginning of Zedekiah's reign. This is the short but significant time of Jehoiachin, son of Jehoiakim, who sat upon Judah's throne for three months and ten days.

The death of Jehoiakim is clouded in mystery. When he withheld tribute from Babylon, Nebuchadnezzar sent troops to discipline the stubborn vassal. The country was overrun and reduced to wretchedness, poverty, misery, and confusion. In the events that followed, Jehoiakim's life came to an end, probably in a violent manner. Kittel concludes, "Jehoiakim's sudden death saves him from a bitter humiliation."

Jehoiachin inherited the unattractive situation. After a brief period, the young monarch surrendered to Babylon. He, his mother Nehushta, and the "flower of the land" were deported to the distant country. Those taken included the warriors, smiths, craftsmen, and nobility. "None remained, save the poorest . . . of the land" (2 Kings 24:14).

There are two short oracles which date from the brief reign of Jehoiachin. Each of these fragments is located in a larger section which was compiled for topical reasons. The material in 22:1 to 23:8 is, as mentioned before, a collection of Jeremiah's messages to each of the kings concerning their administration of national affairs. In 22:24–30 there is a sermon addressed to Jehoiachin. The prophet warned the king of coming captivity and further declared that no seed of Jehoiachin should sit upon the throne of Judah. There is good reason to believe that this message influenced Jehoiachin in his decision to surrender to Babylon. The other recorded word of Jeremiah dating from Jehoiachin's reign is a dirge on the approaching doom (13:18–27). It appears in the same chapter with two other oracles, all of which deal with the subject of Judah's pride. This thirteenth chapter is a compilation and has a unity of subject matter rather than a unity of chronological sequence. This brief oracle also exerted an influence on the young king in his decision to capitulate to Nebuchadnezzar.

With the coming of Zedekiah to the throne, Judah's afternoon shadows lengthened quickly into twilight. Zedekiah was the third son of Josiah to rule and was a brother of Jehoahaz and Jehoiakim. He immediately bound himself by an oath to serve Babylon. It is interesting to observe that each of the three sons of Josiah were sponsored by a different political group. Jehoahaz had been placed on the throne by the nationalists of Judah, Jehoiakim had been sponsored by Pharaoh Necho and the pro-Egyptian party in Judah, while Zedekiah was a protégé of the Babylonian king.

The last two outstanding kings of Judah, though brothers,

were a distinct contrast in personality. Jehoiakim was stubborn and self-willed. His every thought seemed a determination to do evil. Zedekiah, however, from all appearances, wanted to do that which was right. His deficiency of character lay in his inability to do what his better self told him was for his country's political and spiritual welfare. He was vacillating and weak-kneed, running first to one group and then to another. He seemed utterly incapable of making a decision and standing by it. As he began reigning, he took an oath of allegiance to Babylon, but the pro-Egyptian party in Judah would not let him enjoy peace of mind. Rather than fulfil his vow and hold fast his loyalty to Babylon, he sought to determine which course was politically expedient. This policy eventually resulted in national suicide.

During the early years of Zedekiah's reign Jeremiah's task was twofold. He sought to convince the people who remained in Judah that the future of the Jewish nation lay in those who had been carried into captivity. They who were captives in Babylon were the "good figs" of chapter 24, while those who remained in Judah were the "bad figs." The other mission of Jeremiah was to warn the people in Babylon that the captivity would last a long time. There would be no speedy return. He wrote a letter to the captives (chap. 29) in which he instructed them, "Build ye houses, and dwell in them; and plant gardens, and eat the fruit of them. Take ye wives, and beget sons and daughters. . . . And seek the peace of the city whither I have caused you to be carried away captive" (29:5–7).

These two sections (chaps. 24 and 29) give a picture of Jeremiah as he pleaded with the people to adjust themselves to the changes of life that had been brought about because of Babylon's entrance upon Judah's national life, bringing poverty to the homeland and taking captives to Babylon. There are some spiritual lessons the prophet was seeking to teach.

Never Forsaken

Israel was holiness unto the Lord. He taught her to walk (Hos. 11:3), bore her on eagle's wings, and brought her to himself (Ex. 19:4). But her choice citizens became captives. They hung their harps upon the willows and sought to sing the Lord's song in a strange land. Sitting by the rivers of Babylon, they could only weep as they remembered Zion (Psalm 137:1–2).

This letter to the exiles gives us a keen insight into the character of Jeremiah. Early in his ministry he had shouted a flaming warning to his people: "Thine own wickedness shall correct thee, and thy backslidings shall reprove thee" (2:19). The preacher had been vindicated. His earlier ministry was of the Lord. It had come to pass even as the boy prophet had foretold. The great heart of the prophet is revealed as he turns immediately to a message of hope and comfort. The exiles were to recognize that God would not leave them. They were still his people. Because they had been rebellious it was necessary for them to be disciplined, but there is always a future for failures. It was to the exiles in Babylon that the ever-comforting words were spoken: "Ye shall seek me, and find me, when ye shall search for me with all your heart" (29:13). God knew his thoughts toward his people. It was his purpose to bring them peace and not evil. Jehovah would turn again their captivity and gather them from all nations; he would bring them again unto the place from which he caused them to be carried away captive (29:11, 14).

But Israel must learn a great lesson. She was not to listen to false optimists. There were seventy years of captivity for her. During this time she must keep the fires of spiritual religion burning. The false prophets in her midst would endeavor to lead the people astray, but Jehovah warned, "Let not your prophets that are in the midst of you, and your diviners, deceive you; neither hearken ye to your dreams which ye cause to be dreamed" (29:8).

In every age God's people must learn these truths of patience and trust. Elijah was reminded under the juniper trees that there were still seven thousand who had not bowed their knees to Baal (1 Kings 19:18). The prophets of doom never failed to remind their people of a glorious day of redemption and restoration. Amos spoke of the day of the Lord as "darkness, and not light" (5:18), but he also saw another day in the future when God's blessings should be so evident that "the plowman shall overtake the reaper, and the treader of grapes him that soweth seed; and the mountains shall drop sweet wine, and all the hills shall melt" (9:13). During the darkest days of the Reformation the wife of Martin Luther had to remind the great man of God with a striking object lesson that "God is not dead." The Pharaohs, Benhadads, Sennacheribs, and Nebuchadnezzars have strutted across the pages of history, but God is still alive and is still on the throne. Because he is alive his people are never forsaken.

The book of Esther, written against the backdrop of Babylonian captivity, reveals as does no other piece of literature the protecting hand of God. Although the name of God does not appear in the book, his overshadowing presence hovers around every scene. Mordecai reminded Esther in the crisis, "If thou altogether holdest thy peace at this time, then will relief and deliverance arise to the Jews from another place" (Esther 4:14). Moses spoke of "the everlasting arms" (Deut. 33:27), Isaiah of "an everlasting rock" (26:4), and the psalmist of "a refuge and strength, a very present help in trouble" (46:1). The psalmist continued, "Therefore will we not fear, though the earth do change, and though the mountains be shaken into the heart of the seas" (46:2). One of the greatest doctrines in the New Testament is the security of God's child. Thus the hymn writer speaks for God:

> The soul that on Jesus hath leaned for repose,
> I will not, I will not desert to his foes;
> That soul, though all hell should endeavor to shake,
> I'll never, no, never, no, never forsake!

Never Defeated

When Abraham was called to leave the cosmopolitan capital of the Chaldees, God purposed to lead his seed until the fulness of time should bring forth Him who was to be a blessing to all families of the earth. The spiritual life of Israel did not always maintain the highest level. Sometimes God chose to step across the line into Gentile circles to continue the messianic strain, but in every action God was "working a work" (Hab. 1:5). Jeremiah's letter to the exiles expressed confidence that God's purposes would ultimately succeed regardless of what the years might bring of spiritual adversity. Jeremiah would agree with Tennyson,

> Yet I doubt not thro' the ages one increasing purpose runs,
> And the thoughts of men are widen'd with the process of the suns.

Chapter 24 contains Jeremiah's vision in Jerusalem of two baskets of figs: "One basket had very good figs, like the figs that are first-ripe; and the other basket had very bad figs, which could not be eaten, they were so bad" (v. 2). Jeremiah used this symbolism to convey an important truth to those in Jerusalem. God's purpose would continue but not through those left in the homeland. The good figs were those people who were in Babylon. God had set his eyes upon them for good. He would bring them back to Judah. He would build them up and not pull them down. He would plant them and not pluck them up. The evil figs were those people remaining in the land. They would be driven to faraway kingdoms. They would become a reproach and a proverb, a taunt and a curse in all the places where they were driven (24:9).

Jeremiah thus had a message for both groups of Judah's citizens. The people who remained in Judah were warned against being too optimistic. The captives in Babylon were comforted against being too pessimistic. Jeremiah made it clear to both groups that God's eternal purpose would be worked out through the small remnant in Babylon. Concerning the captives, God spoke through Jeremiah: "And I will give them a heart to know me, that I am Jehovah: and they shall be my people, and I will be their God; for they shall return unto me with their whole heart" (24:7). Isaiah's classic doctrine of the remnant is once more an important part of God's plan.

In the midst of a noisy world which places a premium on bigness we need constantly to keep before us the fact that God does not always work with the spectacular, the glamorous, and the obvious. We need also to remember that when God's purposes seem most frustrated, he is often most at work.

Take, for instance, the year 1809. It was one of the most discouraging in the history of Europe. One writer predicted that future generations would call it "the world's blackest year." Napoleon was dominating the Continent and making plans for further conquest. The cause of freedom and social progress seemed doomed. But God was at work. In that year Abraham Lincoln, William Gladstone, Alfred Tennyson, Edgar Allan Poe, Oliver Wendell Holmes, Cyrus Hall McCormick, and Felix Mendelssohn were born. That year was not as hopeless as it seemed.

In 1812 the United States was engaged in a great conflict with England. Most of the American coast was blockaded, and morale was at a low ebb. This same year, however, the American Foreign Mission movement was begun as Adoniram Judson and Luther Rice set sail for Burma. From 1861 to 1865 the Civil War threatened the destruction of American economic, educational, and spiritual stakes. Yet during those days God was at work planning for a better nation, and there were born such men as George Washington Carver, Charles Mayo, Charles Steinmetz, Henry Ford, John Pershing, and Billy Sunday. Those who have the deeper wisdom believe God is working most when he is least seen and felt.

Never Limited

One of the greatest deficiencies of the people in the ancient world was a limited conception of God. Each of the pagan tribes had its own deity, and this god's rule was circumscribed to that particular area. This religious thinking of the pagan world had been somewhat absorbed into much of the popular thinking of Israel and Judah. This may have been in the background of Jonah's mind as he "rose up to flee unto Tarshish from the presence of Jehovah" (Jonah 1:3).

It was the mission of the canonical prophets to keep before the people the fact that Jehovah was more than a tribal god whose presence was limited to Zion and who could be worshiped only in Jerusalem. Most of the prophetical books have a section of prophecies concerning countries other than Israel. The purpose of these foreign prophecies was to remind the people that Jehovah's rule was not limited to one country. God's moral law as well as his love extends to all people. It was not easy for the prophets to convince the people of the universality of their God. They longed to be like the other nations, and they therefore found it easy to adopt the concept of a god who was interested in their welfare exclusively. Their limited view of God is a partial explanation of Judah's intense nationalism and lack of missionary zeal during Old Testament days.

It is always difficult to enlarge an individual's concept of his god. J. B. Phillips says, "The trouble with many people today is they have not found a God big enough for modern needs. While their experience of life has grown in a score of directions, and their mental horizons have been expanded to the point of bewilderment by world events and by scientific discoveries, their ideas of God have remained largely static." Many times in counseling with adults who are having difficulty concerning their religious faith one can only say, "Your problem is you have outgrown childish ideas of God but have never adopted mature concepts." The results of such a dilemma is an inner dissatisfaction caused by a religious vacuum. As one grows in years, he must worship and serve a God who is big enough to command his highest admiration and his adult loyalty. Jeremiah was telling the captives that Jehovah is not limited. He was present in Babylon, and they might seek him and find him an even greater God than they ever before realized when they seek him with all their heart.

Never Static

The fundamental law of life is growth. Gibbons said, "All that is human must retrograde if it does not advance." Victor Hugo spoke of progress as "the onward strides of God." A famous football coach declared, "The best defense is a good offense," while Ralph Waldo Emerson said, "Progress is the activity of today, and the assurance of tomorrow."

In the kingdom of God the basic principle is spiritual growth. A person does not suddenly become mature in the initial experience of the Christian life called regeneration. Peter admonished his readers to "grow in the grace and knowledge" (2 Peter 3:18). Paul assured the Philippians that "he which hath begun a good work in you will go on developing it until the day of Jesus Christ" (Phil. 1:6, author's translation). The author of Hebrews urged his readers to "press on unto perfection" (6:1). The Sermon on the Mount may well be summarized in one statement, "Be ye therefore perfect [full grown], even as your Father which is in heaven is perfect" (Matt. 5:48, AV).

In many ways Jeremiah and Jesus were alike. The most distinctive parallel was in their agreement on the necessity for moving onward with God. Jesus is the "pioneer of life" who constantly challenges his people to enlarge their horizons and enter new fields of Christian service. The world is not going backward. God's program will not stand still nor remain static. A better translation of Hebrews 2:1 would be, "We ought to give the more earnest heed to the things which we have heard *lest perchance we be passed by.*" A tragic sight in a church program or any kingdom endeavor is to see someone or some group who will not grow and hence is "passed by." Charles M. Crowe says, "When we stop breaking new

117

ground, life goes stale." He says further that in every realm of life this is true. Take, for instance, the Pierce-Arrow automobile. In 1910 the name alone was valued at a million dollars. The company, however, did not keep pace with new developments in the automotive industry. Today the name is worthless. No manufacturer wants it for any price. This is always the penalty when one refuses to grow.

The life that continues to advance remains vital and useful to the end. When Longfellow was past seventy, he was asked for the secret of his youthful spirit and energy. He pointed to a nearby tree with blossoms and said, "I try to be like that tree, I grow a little new wood every year." Tennyson was eighty when he wrote "Crossing the Bar." Robert Louis Stevenson left an unfinished novel, "Weir of Hermiston," when he died. The story breaks off in the middle of a sentence which the author had written on the morning of his death. Whittier's last poem, and one of his most beautiful, "To Oliver Wendell Holmes," was written but a few weeks before his death. Charles Dickens was working on what promised to be his best novel when he died. This is the purpose and pattern of the Christian life. Let it be full and useful to the very end.

Across the centuries the prophet speaks to our hearts. God's people are never forsaken, God's purposes are never defeated, God's presence is never limited, and God's program is never static. "New occasions teach new duties." Let us learn to adjust to new circumstances, rejoice in new responsibilities, and utilize new opportunities.

10

"But Thou, O Man of God"

Any attempt to evaluate the life and ministry of Jeremiah would be inadequate without an examination of his attitude toward, and relationship with, the other prophets of his day. A study of the book reveals that the word "prophet" or some form of this word appears in it more than in any other of the Old Testament books. The word "prophet" is used forty-three times, the plural "prophets" fifty-one times, "prophesied" fifteen times, "prophesieth" one time, and "prophesy" twenty-two times. This makes a total of ninety-four times as a noun and thirty-eight times as a verb. Jeremiah was first, last, and always a prophet of God. He was ordained a "prophet to the nations," and throughout each epoch of his life until he went finally to Egypt he was "Jeremiah the prophet."

There is, however, a distinct contrast between Jeremiah of Anathoth and the false prophets who were his contemporaries. It is true that the Old Testament Scriptures nowhere use the expression "false prophet," but this is the term Old Testament students have agreed upon to designate these men who claimed to have a message from Jehovah but who were in direct opposition to the preaching and policy of such men as Jeremiah. The suggestion probably came from the

119

words of Jesus, who spoke several times of "false prophets" and described them as those which "come to you in sheep's clothing, but inwardly they are ravening wolves" (Matt. 7:15).

At the beginning of his ministry the youthful preacher referred to the false prophets with such statements as "the prophets prophesied by Baal" (2:8), "the prophets prophesy falsely" (5:31), and "the prophet . . . dealeth falsely. . . . saying, Peace, peace; when there is no peace" (6:13-14). It was not until the early years of Zedekiah's reign, however, that the real clash came between Jeremiah and these false prophets. The historical material which deals with this conflict is found in chapters 27 and 28. Another passage, 23:9-40, is a discourse against the false prophets which was delivered during this general period and added to the compiled material in 22:1 to 23:8 to make a collection of messages concerning the kings and prophets of Judah. An examination of this material will lay a foundation for a further study of prophecy.

Many students regard chapters 27-29 as a section of Jeremianic material which at one time had a separate existence before being incorporated into the present book of Jeremiah. It has been called "The Roll of the Early Reign of Zedekiah." The marginal note on 27:1 is undoubtedly correct, and we should read "Zedekiah" instead of "Jehoiakim." Chapters 27 and 28 are inseparably connected and should be regarded as in much the same relation as the two chapters (7 and 26) dealing with the temple sermon. Chapter 27 deals with the prophet's attitude toward the false prophets collectively, while chapter 28 records Jeremiah's encounter with an individual representative of the order.

In the early years of Zedekiah's reign there began a movement among the various nations to form a coalition against Babylon. A new king had also ascended the throne of Egypt. It seemed an ideal time for Judah, Egypt, Tyre, Sidon, Ammon, Moab, and Edom to pool their strength against the rising nation. Messengers were sent to Jerusalem to persuade Zedekiah to join the group. Jeremiah's attitude toward the alliance is revealed in this chapter. It was the will of Jehovah that Babylon shall rule the nations for a period of time. Jeremiah represented God as speaking of Babylon as "my servant." The nation which recognized Babylon as being the agent of Jehovah for this period would be wise, but the one who sought to revolt against her power would die by the sword, famine, and pestilence (27:13). The false prophets were telling the people Babylon would fall shortly and were encouraging a rebellion against Nebuchadnezzar. Jeremiah's position was firm. Babylon would stand secure. The captives would not return, but others of Judah would also go into captivity. The people must not hearken to the false prophets.

Chapter 28 contains the account of a personal clash between Jeremiah and Hananiah. The latter was insistent in his contention that Babylon's power would be broken within two years. His message was so confidently delivered that momentarily it seemed he had convinced Jeremiah. After a conference with Jehovah, however, Jeremiah returned to Hananiah with a fresh message. The Lord would substitute yokes of iron for the yokes of wood which Hananiah had broken. Hananiah was making the people trust in a lie. Babylon would not fall shortly. The nations must be her servant as long as Jehovah decreed. Because of his false message, Hananiah would die within a year. Two months later the false prophet died.

These passages give an excellent foundation for a discussion of Old Testament prophecy. The history of Israel is bound inseparably with that of the prophets. God's activity in the world went hand in hand with his revelation to and through the prophets. Amos avowed, "Surely the Lord Jehovah will do nothing, except he reveal his secret unto his servants the prophets" (3:7).

The Prophetic Movement

In his *Introducing the Old Testament* Clyde Francisco says, "The roll call of the prophets of Israel includes the most illustrious heroes of her history, from Abraham . . . to Jesus." There is a sense in which every one of God's leaders are prophets inasmuch as the word *navi,* which is translated "prophet," comes from a Hebrew root meaning "to speak." Thus in the larger context anyone who speaks for God is a prophet of God. It is, therefore, quite accurate to designate Abraham (Gen. 20:7) and Moses (Deut. 34:10) as prophets and even to include prophetesses such as Miriam (Ex. 15:20) and Deborah (Judg. 4:4) in the noble succession.

There existed during the history of Israel, however, a line of ecstatic prophets with a strong tendency toward nationalism. This group seems to have begun shortly after the period of the Judges and flourished during the days of Samuel, Elijah, and Elisha. With the coming of the canonical prophets of the eighth and seventh centuries B.C. these ecstatics seem to grow less prevalent or to disappear completely; but some would cite Ezekiel as an exception.

One of the greatest tasks of Bible students is to determine the true history of the prophetic movement. There are two main suggestions, and the full truth probably lies perhaps between the two schools of thought. The first approach is to consider the true succession of Old Testament prophets as beginning with Abraham and Moses, continuing through the moral and ethical leaders of the nation such as Samuel, Elijah, and Elisha, and culminating in Isaiah, Hosea, Jeremiah, Habakkuk, and their canonical contemporaries. The others would be outside the prophetic stream except for a few of the minor figures such as Micaiah and Nathan, who were bold to stand for ethical righteousness against political and numerical opposition.

The other approach is to see prophecy as a developmental process. The prophet was originally called a seer (1 Sam. 9:9). The roots of the prophetic movement are connected with priestly diviners, dreams, ephods, and ecstatic trances. The earlier prophets were ultrapatriotic. To them Jehovah was the unconditional ally of Israel regardless of the spiritual quality of her national life. As time moved on, however, prophecy took on an ethical coloring. The eighth century saw the full flower of prophetic thought with a moral insight never before reached by the earlier movement.

When there are two contrasting schools of thought, the truth is usually somewhere between the two extremes. There seems no doubt that Abraham and Moses were regarded as prophets. On the other hand, Samuel, Elijah, and Elisha, who are certainly to be recognized as true prophets, were connected in some definite way with the ecstatic groups of their day. There is some support for the contention that the "false prophets" of Jeremiah's day and a bit earlier were at least to some extent a carry-over from the nationalistic ecstatics who were ultra-optimistic concerning Judah's destiny. The true prophet, on the other hand, believed in Judah's political safety only if she remained morally right. Even as one of America's statesmen said, "Nothing is politically right which is morally wrong," so the true prophet of Jehovah believed that the ultimate security of a nation lay in its spiritual strength.

A. B. Davidson's position is one of the best summaries of the prophetic movement to be found. According to him, "The line of prophetic teachers has been uninterrupted since the days of Moses." He says, "The real history of Israel is a history in which men of prophetic rank and name stand at the great turning-points of the people's life, and direct the movements." [1] Jeremiah would agree with this interpretation of prophecy, for he declared, "Since the day that your fathers came forth out of the land of Egypt unto this day, I have sent unto you all my servants the prophets" (7:25).

Informed students declare with unanimity that the prophetic movement was the greatest influence ever exerted in the world. Carl Cornill, the German scholar, said, "The whole history of mankind has nothing that can be compared in the remotest degree with the prophecy of Israel," and he spoke of Hebrew prophecy as "one of the greatest spiritual forces that the history of mankind has ever witnessed." [2] Gordon claims, "It may be safely asserted that the prophetic succession was the specific contribution of Israel to the world." In the fourth century of Christianity Athanasius, staunch defender of the faith, testified to the universality of the prophetic influence, "For indeed it was not for the sake of the Jews alone that the prophets were sent. . . . but for the whole world they were a sacred school of knowledge concerning God and spiritual life."

The prophetic movement began the spiritual history of the world. Each age has its representatives in the noble succession. According to one scholar, "Jesus of Nazareth linked His own activity to the prophecy of ancient Israel, Himself the purest blossom and fairest flower."

124

God of the prophets! Bless the prophets' sons:
  Elijah's mantle o'er Elisha cast;
Each age its solemn task may claim but once:
  Make each one nobler, stronger than the last!
                                DENIS WORTMAN

The Prophetic Message

Perhaps the most debated subject of Old Testament study is that of prophecy. Unfortunately the lines of theological thinking are divided sharply at this point.

The most popular concept of prophecy is, of course, that which magnifies the predictive element. The average person would say that a prophet is one who predicts the future. This is, in fact, about as far as most people go in their thinking. The best approach is a cautious one, avoiding extremity in either direction. There are, to be sure, examples of predictive prophecy in the Old Testament. One who denies this is not fair with the evidence. On the other hand, however, one who confines his definition of prophecy to the foretelling of future events or who sees the predictive element as the major emphasis of prophecy has missed the heart of the prophetic message.

The prophets may best be understood as "forth-tellers." They declared the will of God in great moral and spiritual principles. The message which they spoke was primarily to their own generation. Fearlessly, yet lovingly, they spoke in terms of the spiritual needs of their day. Their message must always be interpreted in light of the historical background, and yet, because they spoke in eternal principles, their message is timeless and thus relevant for all generations.

One of the chief tasks of the prophet is to interpret for his people the character of God. The cry of the human race has always been for a revelation of the Infinite. These men of God represent the highest peak of Old Testament revelation and give the most adequate picture of God possible until Jesus of Nazareth stepped into history and the Word became flesh. Every New Testament doctrine lies in embryo within the prophetic messages. The prophets need only for Jesus to demonstrate and the Holy Spirit to breathe on their messages for them to be fully Christian.

Each of the Old Testament prophets gave his own emphasis concerning the nature of God. These emphases are not contradictory but supplementary. Isaiah magnified the holiness of God; Amos, the justice; Hosea, the love and mercy. Micah set forth the ethical content of the divine character, while Jonah gave a picture of the universal nature of God's concern and compassion. The unique contribution of Jeremiah is that God may be known in personal fellowship apart from the intensive machinery of the legalized religion of his day. The preacher in any day who interprets God in terms of moral character and ethical righteousness is in the prophetic succession.

The true prophet of God seeks to lead his people to a fuller understanding of the true meaning of sin. It is his duty to redefine sin to a nation that had lost consciousness of its deeper implications. One's concept of sin is always relative to his concept of God. The nature of sin is colored by the nature of the Deity against whom the sin is committed. If one conceives of God as one who will be satisfied with burnt offerings, year-old calves, and rivers of oil, then failure to observe these technical requirements is sin. But if one sees religion as a relationship between a God of character and a man who in loving obedience seeks to live in and maintain fellowship with this God, then sin is any act or attitude which disrupts or severs this relationship. To the prophets, and especially to Jeremiah and Hosea, sin was not merely transgression against law but also against love. It is essentially inward, and therefore its greatest effect is the mark it leaves on the individual, destroying his character and driving a wedge between him and fellowship with his God. Sin produces its own punishment. Jeremiah said, "Thine own wickedness shall correct thee" (2:19). We are not only punished for our sins, but the moral law of God also makes certain that we are punished by our sins.

Again, the prophets are incurable optimists. This does not mean that they compromise with sin. Neither does it mean that they minimize its effect upon the individual or upon society. It means rather that they see beyond the limitations of the present to a time when God's will shall be done on earth as it is being done in heaven. God reminded Habakkuk, "I am working a work" (1:5). This was in many ways the characteristic philosophy of the Old Testament prophet.

Jeremiah never forgot the assurance given to him at the outset of his ministry, "I watch over my word to perform it" (1:12). To the true prophet of God the greatest heresy conceivable is an attempt to divorce God from the activities of history. During the days of Hezekiah, when Rabshakeh was presenting his arguments as to why Jerusalem should surrender to Sennacherib, Isaiah remained silent until Rabshakeh questioned the ability of God to act in history. The Assyrian propaganda agent dared to suggest that Jehovah was no stronger than the gods of Hamath and Arpad, who had not been able to save the people who trusted in them (Isa. 36:19). It was then that Isaiah announced the coming judgment upon the Assyrian forces.

Twentieth-century prophets of God must likewise believe

127

in the coming kingdom of God. It is not enough to see gloom and doom; it is wrong to adopt the escapist philosophy that Jesus will bring the kingdom and therefore we are not obligated to work for social righteousness. Any scheme for the reconstruction of society which ignores individual redemption is untenable, but any doctrine of personal salvation which does not seek to enlist redeemed sinners in the work of extending the kingdom of God in the hearts of men is equally untenable. Clyde V. Hickerson says, "It is not a matter of choice between preaching a Gospel to individuals or bringing a message that challenges every institution that bars the way to mankind's highest welfare. We are to do both. Ours is not a restricted program of 'either one or the other,' but 'both one and the other.'"

The Prophetic Man

Truth will bless the world only as it becomes incarnate. Phillips Brooks's classic definition of preaching, "the communication of truth through personality," is illustrated superlatively in the life of the Hebrew prophets.

Emerson's challenge, "What you are speaks so loudly I cannot hear what you say"; Francis of Assisi telling his young student, "We were preaching while we were walking. We have been seen by many. Our behavior has been closely watched . . . It is no use, my son, walking anywhere to preach unless you preach as you walk"; and the modern poet who said, "I'd rather see a sermon than hear one any day"— all these remind us that the most important thing about a prophet of God, whether in ancient Israel or in the twentieth century, is the quality of his spiritual life as revealed in the depth of his personal character. It was not merely the message of the Hebrew prophet that distinguished him from his contemporaries. The true spokesman for God had basic traits of character that set him apart. His life was a distinct contrast in all areas to those who "prophesied by Baal, and caused . . . Israel to err" (23:13).

The man of God is conscious of a personal call. There may be some things about a prophet that are optional, but it is essential that he be sent from God. In the crises of life he can go back to his call and draw strength from the conviction that he is in the Lord's service because of the imperative summons of the eternal God. Jowett said, "The call of the Eternal must ring through the rooms of his soul as clearly as the sound of the morning-bell rings through the valleys of Switzerland, calling the peasants to early prayer and praise. . . . His choice is not a preference among alternatives. Ultimately he has no alternative . . ."

The false prophets have no such consciousness. In Jeremiah's day they spoke a vision of their own hearts, "not out of the mouth of Jehovah" (23:16). The Lord "sent not these prophets, yet they ran." He "spake not unto them, yet they prophesied." If they had stood in his council, then would they have caused the people to hear God's words and would have turned the people from their evil ways (23:21–22). The prophets who have no call have no message. They can only steal their message from their neighbors (23:30). They can only prophesy lying dreams and cause the people to err by their vain boastings. The Lord "sent them not, nor commanded them; neither do they profit this people" (23:32).

The true prophet has an experience of call to which he can return in his moments of discouragement and despondency. Many scholars believe that the reason Isaiah's call is placed in chapter 6 rather than in chapter 1 is because he had preached for a short period of time, and the people were not heeding his message. In his extremity, and in order to persuade the people as well as perhaps to reassure himself that he was called of God, he described the inaugural vision which ushered him into the prophetic ministry. Although Amos did mention his call briefly in the second chapter, it was not until the latter part of his book, when Amaziah challenged his message, that Amos told of his call experience, saying, "I was no prophet, neither was I a prophet's son; but I was a herdsman, and a dresser of sycomore-trees: and Jehovah took me from following the flock, and Jehovah said unto me, Go, prophesy unto my people Israel" (7:14–15). The greater the prophet's consciousness of a divine call, the greater will be his authority, and all other things being equal, the greater his effectiveness as a divine messenger.

The true prophet is a man of unimpeachable integrity, delivering the truth as it has been revealed to him regardless of personal desires or ambitions. The false prophet is a man of doubtful character, sometimes actually immoral. He is a time-server, preaching a pleasing and optimistic message at all times in order to be popular and win praise from his hearers. Jeremiah spoke in scathing terms concerning these false prophets. His heart was broken within, and all his bones shook as he viewed the sinfulness of the land (23:9). He placed the blame upon the religious leaders who were profane. Their wickedness was found even in the house of the Lord (23:11). They prophesied by Baal and caused the people to err. In the prophets Jeremiah had seen a horrible thing: "They commit adultery, and walk in lies; and they strengthen the hands of evil-doers, so that none doth return from his wickedness" (23:14).

There must be always uppermost in the prophet's mind the sacredness of his calling. This divine setting-apart calls for a nobility of character unequaled by any other field of service or vocation. The message of the prophet is important, but it is his character which vindicates his message and validates his calling.

Finally, the true prophet in any age is conscious of the ethical and moral character of God and the corresponding demand for such character in the lives of God's people. The New Testament refers frequently to believers as "sons of God." One of the basic concepts of the word "son" both in the Old and New Testaments is "one who possesses like characteristics." John Milton once said, "He who would not be frustrated of his hope to write well ought himself to be a true poem."

An incident from the life of John Wesley may summarize the description of a prophet. Wesley was preaching in the slums of a large city to a crowd gathered on the street. There were two tramps standing not far from the preacher. One picked up a jagged rock and started to hurl it at Wesley's face. His arm was in the air, prepared to loose the rock, when his eyes suddenly met those of Wesley. The light of God's love reflected in the prophet's eyes and shone in his face. The tramp dropped the rock, turned to his buddy and said, "Look at his face, bo, look at his face! He ain't a man, he's a god!" Wesley finished his sermon, dismissed the audience, and passed through the crowd. He passed the tramp, patted him on the shoulder, and said, "God bless you, my man, God bless you." As Wesley made his way through the crowd, the tramp turned back to his buddy and then pointed to Wesley. Half to himself and half aloud, he said, "I was wrong, bo, he ain't a god, he's a man—but he's a man like God!"

A prophet is a man of God who, through his message, his morals, and his manhood, leads others to accept God.

11

"A Correspondence Fixed with Heaven"

The Scottish poet Robert Burns has blessed the world with many gems of thought, but nowhere does he give greater spiritual truth than in these words:

A correspondence fixed with Heaven
Is sure a noble anchor.

It is always dangerous to deal in superlatives, but perhaps the most significant fact in the life and ministry of Jeremiah was that he possessed a most unusual fellowship with the Infinite. No other prophet conversed so intimately with God, and no other dared to speak so frankly and so boldly.

A partial explanation may be found in the type of life which the prophet pursued. Jeremiah's existence was a lonely one. He had no wife and family to undergird his ministry. He was misunderstood even by his closest friends. His fellow townsmen tried to kill him, and his own kinsmen joined the conspiracy. The prophets of his day were aligned against him and preached a message diametrically opposed to his own. He was forced to flee and remain in hiding in order to escape death at the hands of the king. His only fellowship was with

God, and he was conscious in a very unusual way of the presence of the Lord. Because of this, he spoke to God in a manner which to us seems bold and familiar, but for him it was most natural.

An important portion of Scripture deals with Jeremiah's personal relationship with Jehovah. The "Confessions of Jeremiah" were mentioned in chapter 4 but were not discussed fully. This division may be called "A Correspondence in Confusion." Jeremiah's activity during the siege of Jerusalem will be entitled "A Correspondence in a Crisis." Finally, the ministry of Jeremiah after the fall of Jerusalem and the burning of the Temple will be designated "A Correspondence in Calamity."

A Correspondence in Confusion

There is scattered throughout the book of Jeremiah a group of poetical passages which present a picture of Jeremiah's life not given by the other material. Old Testament students have agreed to call these "The Confessions of Jeremiah." It is also generally accepted by scholars that these units formed no part of his public message but recorded the prophet's inner spiritual battles. In them is exhibited the prophet's personal communion with God. There are shown his prayer life, his longings, doubts, fears, and mental conflicts, but also his faith in God's eternal purposes. Jeremiah was moody and dared to ask "why" of the Almighty, but Jeremiah was no pessimist. No true prophet of God is ever a pessimist. He became confused because of contemporary problems, but his redemption was his "correspondence fixed with Heaven." He talked it out with God, and like Jacob of old, he would not let go until he had received a blessing.

These confessions bear different dates, but they fall generally within the middle period of Jeremiah's life. With one exception, they record events during the years of Jehoiakim's wicked reign. These were the days of Jeremiah's greatest confusion. Josiah was dead, and the land was swinging back to the sins which had flourished during the days of Manasseh. Jeremiah was perplexed. At one time he thought the great reformation had solved Judah's moral and spiritual dilemma. The same fickle multitude, however, which had followed Josiah's religious reforms was enthusiastically following Jehoiakim in moral apostasy. Jeremiah was forced to fight a terrific internal battle lest he lose his faith in mankind.

The first section (11:18 to 12:6) of these passages dates from the reign of Josiah. The background of Jeremiah's problem was his preaching tour to Anathoth and the plot against his life by the men of his home town. In some way God had revealed to Jeremiah that they were seeking to kill him, and he was able to escape. The young prophet was confused because of this attempt on his life. He demanded of God why the wicked should prosper and he, a young prophet trying to do God's will, should suffer.

This is, of course, a normal reaction of youth. A young preacher is too often convinced that because he has dedicated himself to God's work all his personal sufferings and problems should be immediately eliminated. It is not long, however, before he discovers that life is not so simple. Adversity may have slain its thousands, but prosperity has slain its tens of thousands. Adversity is needed to develop character. God did not answer Jeremiah directly as to the value of suffering in the development of strong moral and spiritual fiber, but he made it plain that this was only the beginning. "If thou hast run with the footmen, and they have wearied thee, then how canst thou contend with horses? and though in a land of peace thou art secure, yet how wilt thou do in the swelling of the Jordan?" (12:5, margin).

God revealed further that it was worse than Jeremiah thought. The young prophet had been condemning the men of Anathoth for seeking his life. (The section 11:18 to 12:4 contains the words of Jeremiah to God. The verses 12:5–6 are the answer of God to Jeremiah.) God told Jeremiah that the prophet's own family was a part of the conspiracy. Charles Edward Jefferson summarized God's answer to Jeremiah in these words, "Cheer up, the worst is yet to come." In modern parlance we would say, "Things are going to get a lot worse before they start getting better."

The second and third sections, from a chronological standpoint, are 18:18–23 and 20:7–18. Both of these passages are a part of the roll concerning the potter and his work (chaps. 18–20) and represent the earlier period of Jehoiakim's reign while there still seemed to be hope for national repentance. Jeremiah was seeking through symbolic messages to lead the people to spiritual transformation rather than legalistic reformation. The beautiful story of the visit to the potter's house and Jeremiah's plea to the people concerning their spiritual need is recorded in 18:1–17. The remainder of the chapter (vv. 18–23) consists of Jeremiah's complaint to God that his enemies have digged a pit for his soul even though he has interceded for them and his imprecatory prayer that God will vindicate him by destroying those who "smite him with the tongue" and "devise devices against him." The other confession in the roll of the potter follows 19:1 to 20:6 and shows the reflections of Jeremiah after Pashhur had put him in stocks for preaching of coming captivity and after the people had taunted him for naming Babylon as the coming instrument of God's judgment.

The two final confessions (15:10–21 and 17:9–18) come earlier in the book but later in the ministry of Jeremiah. Some scholars include 16:1–3 as part of the first of these confessions. All the material in chapters 14–17 should be dated during the latter part of Jehoiakim's ministry, when Judah's fate was virtually sealed because of Jehoiakim's stubborn wickedness. The probable exception is 17:19–27, which dates from Josiah's reign and seems to have been added as an independent message.

The fourth confession takes up where the third one ends. There is evidence of a continuity of thought and development of ideas as these confessions follow one another. In the latter part of the third confession Jeremiah cursed the day of his birth and moaned because he had come forth that his days should be consumed with shame. In the opening of the fourth confession of Jeremiah he was still lamenting his entrance into the world. He called himself a man of strife and contention to the whole earth. There is a touch of humor in his statement, "I have not lent, neither have men lent to me; yet every one of them doth curse me" (15:10). Jeremiah's confusion continued. He rejoiced not in the assembly of those that made merry. He sat alone because of God's hand. It seemed to Jeremiah that God was unto him as a deceitful brook, whose waters fail. The prophet was learning the lesson that prophets in every generation must learn: there is a loneliness for all great servants of God. In 16:1–3 God told Jeremiah that he was not to marry. This intensified his dilemma but led to a closer correspondence with the spiritual.

The final confession (17:9–18) finds the light breaking through at least a part of Jeremiah's confusion. He began to understand that the source of the world's ills is that the heart is deceitful above all things, and it is exceedingly corrupt.

Jeremiah was approaching the great doctrine of individualism which he enunciated so clearly in the new covenant. The prophet showed spiritual progress in these confessions, but he still retained a bitter spirit toward those who opposed him. He demanded that God vindicate him—"Let them be put to shame that persecute me, but let not me be put to shame; let them be dismayed, but let not me be dismayed; bring upon them the day of evil, and destroy them with double destruction" (17:18).

These confessions are valuable for our day. We, too, must fight the fight of faith. The prosperity of the wicked and the seeming failure of the divine message constitute problems for us and lead us to question the essential goodness of God and doubt his ultimate power. It fortifies us spiritually to see this man of God as he struggles for the answer. It is not a sin to doubt. The New Testament, of course, says, "Whatsoever is not of faith is sin," but our doubts may be the steppingstones to a deeper concept of faith than we have previously known. P. J. Bailey says,

> Who never doubted never half believed.
> Where doubt there truth is—'tis her shadow.

In these confessions Jeremiah was on a search for spiritual truth. This quest for truth always begins with honest interrogation. To believe with certainty we must begin with doubting. Our confusions can become certainties. Our doubting of smaller truths can give way to the discovery of larger truths if we maintain a "correspondence fixed with Heaven."

A Correspondence in Crisis

The superlative crisis of Jeremiah's ministry was the siege of Jerusalem. Nebuchadnezzar's army encircled the city and remained, with one brief respite, for more than eighteen months. This was the acid test for Judah and an even more acute trial for her greatest prophet. In a siege the prophet is brought to the level of the people. He shares their dangers and duties, their heartaches and hunger. If his faith does not waver and his judgment remains mature, his opportunities for service are great. George Adam Smith says, "A siege can turn a prophet or quiet thinker into a hero."

There are three accounts of major sieges in the Old Testament, and in each a prophet is the central figure. In the days of Ahab, the Syrians under Benhadad surrounded Samaria. Elisha's calm assurance and wise leadership sustained the people. Isaiah's faith in the inviolability of Zion gave confidence to the citizens of Jerusalem during the Assyrian crisis and the seige by the armies of Sennacherib. But Jeremiah, with a more costly courage, counseled Zedekiah to surrender to Babylon.

This section will deal with Jeremiah's activity during the siege of his beloved city. Because the book is made up of a collection of rolls rather than one chronological writing, it will be necessary to gather material from scattered sources. The reason for Jeremiah's quiet confidence and poise during this period of crisis is his "correspondence fixed with Heaven." Jeremiah was past the period of confusion which had issued forth in the confessions. The spiritual struggle with scepticism had been won. God had revealed that Judah's only safety was in submission and surrender to Babylon. This was, of course, the same policy that Jeremiah had recommended in 597 B.C. when Jehoiachin ascended the throne and faced a similar situation. Zedekiah, however, had no intention of following Jeremiah's counsel.

There are three accounts of interviews between Jeremiah

and Zedekiah during this period. The first (21:1–14) was at the beginning of the siege. Actually, this interview was between Jeremiah and the two messengers, Pashhur and Zephaniah, whom Zedekiah had sent to confer with the prophet at the outset of Babylon's activity against Judah. The king was hopeful that Jeremiah might have a word of encouragement from Jehovah. The prophet had no such word. Those who abided in the city would die by the sword, famine, and pestilence. Only those who surrendered to the Chaldeans would live. Jehovah had chosen Babylon as the instrument of his judgment, and therefore he would fight with an outstretched hand and a strong arm against Judah. The kingdom would no longer have God's protection.

The second interview (34:1–7) occurred during the siege while the fighting was actually in progress. Nebuchadnezzar was making an all-out effort to take the city. The record says, "Nebuchadnezzar king of Babylon, and all his army, and all the kingdoms of the earth that were under his dominion, and all the peoples, were fighting against Jerusalem, and against the cities thereof" (34:1). Only Lachish and Azekah remained in Judah as fortified cities (34:7). The message was the same. Jehovah had determined to give the city into the hands of the king of Babylon. The prophet did, however, hold out hope for Zedekiah personally. He would go to Babylon and die in peace.

The third interview (37:1–10) came during a temporary lifting of the siege. The Egyptian army had come from Egypt and was causing concern to the Babylonian forces. The siege was broken, and Zedekiah hoped this meant the salvation of Jerusalem. He sent two messengers, Jehucal and Zephaniah, to inquire of the prophet. The expression "pray for us" in verse 3 should be understood as an entreaty for direction rather than for deliverance. Jeremiah did not share Zedekiah's optimism. Pharaoh's army (Pharaoh Hophra 590–571 B.C.) would return to Egypt. The city of Jerusalem would be burned. Even though the Chaldeans were smitten and there remained only wounded men, yet they would "rise up every man in his tent, and burn this city with fire" (37:10).

In order to follow the events as they occurred we consider next 34:8–22, which is a rebuke to Judah for the treatment of their slaves. When Nebuchadnezzar's army began the siege of Jerusalem, the Jews became very pious. In order to convince Jehovah of their devotion, they released their slaves. These servants were already due their freedom according to Mosaic legislation (Ex. 21:2; Deut. 15:12). Duhm, a German scholar, thinks there was also a selfish motive in this act. The burden of feeding the slaves would have been great at a time when the normal tillage of the ground was held in abeyance. There may be some truth in Duhm's suggestion, but the words of Jeremiah imply that the release was a boon to the slaves rather than a material advantage to the owners.

During the temporary withdrawal of the Chaldeans to meet Egypt's approaching army, the owners decided to call the slaves back into servitude. This was a violent breach of their oath, and Jeremiah denounced with severity this infamous act. This was not merely social injustice. As Peake points out, "The human wrong would in any case have excited the prophet's burning indignation; but their shameless violation of the sanctities of religion, this flaunting of their God to His face involved them in a still deeper condemnation . . . *their perfidy was aggravated by a blasphemous perjury.*" G. Campbell Morgan calls attention to verse 16 and speaks of the true nature of their sin: "Actually it was the sin of breaking faith with the servants, essentially it was the sin of profaning the name of God."

The crisis of Jeremiah grew progressively worse. The material in 37:11–21 gives a further picture of the treatment he received as a result of his faithful preaching of God's message. According to 37:11–14, Jeremiah, when the Chaldean army was broken up for fear of the Egyptians, went from Jerusalem to the land of Benjamin to transact business concerning his inheritance. He was accused of deserting to the Chaldeans and was arrested. Verses 15–16 tell of his confinement in the house of Jonathan the scribe, and verses 17–20 give the account of a secret visit by Zedekiah to Jeremiah. The king inquired, "Is there any word from Jehovah?" Jeremiah replied, "There is. . . . Thou shalt be delivered into the hand of the king of Babylon" (v. 17).

Let us be fair in our evaluation of Zedekiah. He seems to have believed in the inspiration of Jeremiah, and in his heart he wanted to follow the prophet's counsel. Zedekiah, however, was controlled by a group who were determined to resist Babylon even though it meant Judah's doom. Jeremiah petitioned the king that he not be returned to the house of Jonathan the scribe. Zedekiah commanded that Jeremiah be committed into the court of the guard. He was given a loaf of bread daily until all the bread in the city was gone (37:20–21).

Chapter 38 reveals the extremity of Jeremiah's suffering. This chapter contains his experiences after he was transferred to the court of the guard. The first section (vv. 1–6) tells of Jeremiah's fate in the hands of the princes who removed him from the court of the guard and placed him in a dungeon. Actually, this was a cistern, probably an underground one. There was a deep miry sediment in it instead of water. One scholar has suggested that it was a cesspool. Jeremiah was lowered into this pit, and his feet sank in the mire. The second section (vv. 7–13) records his deliverance by an Ethiopian eunuch. We are not told how Ebed-melech, the eunuch, knew of Jeremiah's peril. Some have suggested that he was told by the women of the king's harem. This sounds logical, although there is no evidence either way. The third section (vv. 14–28) contains the account of an interview between Jeremiah and Zedekiah. At the conclusion of the conference Jeremiah was left in the court of the guard until the day Jerusalem was taken.

At the conclusion of chapter 39 there is a message (vv. 15–18) from Jeremiah to Ebed-melech. The prophet gave the promise of Jehovah that when the city fell the Ethiopian eunuch would be delivered. It is a supplement to the account of the siege, and the location of the passage in the English text is, according to Binns, probably due to the desire of the editor to complete the story of the siege before giving this account of the prophet's benefactor.

The final section dealing with this critical period of Jeremiah's life is found in chapters 32 and 33. The evidence seems thoroughly convincing that chapters 30–33 at one time existed as a separate roll. Old Testament scholars have called it "The Book of Comfort." Without going into the technical arguments for dating the passages, we shall consider chapters 32 and 33 as from the period of the last confinement in the court of the guard and chapters 30 and 31 as from the period immediately after the fall of Jerusalem.

In no other passage in the book do we see such a "correspondence with Heaven" as in this material. Things were dark —darker than they had ever been. Jerusalem was about to fall. In the midst of the crisis Jehovah came to Jeremiah with a message. The cousin of the prophet was coming to him with a request that he buy the piece of property in Anathoth that was a part of the family estate. Jeremiah was to buy it and thus show his faith in the future. One must read chapters 32 and 33 with cognizance of the background before he can appreciate such words as, "For thus saith Jehovah of hosts, the God of Israel: Houses and fields and vineyards shall yet again be bought in this land" (32:15).

The prophetic genius of Jeremiah is shown in his ability to sense the need of his people and minister to that need through his messages. He did not minimize the coming judgment in these chapters, but he saw beyond the midnight of judgment to the dawn of a new day. Chapter 33 was delivered shortly after the preceding one when the situation was even worse. But as the crisis became graver, Jeremiah's messages became more hopeful. Jehovah would indeed let his people go into captivity, but he would also bring deliverance. He would bring the people health and cure. He would reveal to them an abundance of peace and truth. He would cause them to return from captivity and would build them as at the first. He would cleanse them from all their iniquities and would pardon their sins and transgressions (33:6–8). Though the cities were waste, without man and without beast, yet again shall be heard the voice of joy and gladness. There shall be weddings, thanksgivings, and religious services. Shepherds shall once more tend their flocks. God's people shall once more dwell in the land which the Lord gave to them (33:10–11).

To speak a message of comfort and optimism under such adverse circumstances required faith in the future. Jeremiah believed in the future because he believed in a God who is active in history, great in counsel, mighty in work, and for whom nothing is too hard. Although he had driven and scattered people, he had the power and love to restore them and to give them one heart and one way in order that they might fear him and depart not from following him (32:37–40). The secret is that the prophet is willing to wait. Is this not the highest concept of faith? The man of faith is the one who is willing to wait on the Lord for his message to be vindicated. The only man who can afford to wait is the man who is right. The more thoroughly convinced one is that he is right, the more willing he is to wait. One cannot have faith without patience; neither can he have patience without faith, and faith and patience come only when there is a "correspondence fixed with Heaven."

A Correspondence in Calamity

Drained and desolate, Jerusalem's day of destruction finally arrived. The long-delayed stroke fell, and with it came Judah's hour of doom. The city's defense had been stubborn, but because of starvation the garrison was finally weakened. In the fourth month of Zedekiah's eleventh year a breach was made in the walls. The Chaldean generals who were in charge of the attack came in and took their position in the middle gate, that is, between the lower city and the citadel of Zion. The latter portion continued to resist, but it was only for a matter of time.

Zedekiah immediately recognized the futility of further hope for Jerusalem's salvation. Under cover of night he fled. The Chaldeans pursued, and the king was overtaken and captured in the plains of Jericho. He was sent to Nebuchadnezzar, who was at Riblah in Hamath. His sons were slain and his leaders executed. Zedekiah's own eyes were then put out, and he was carried in chains to Babylon. Nebuzaradan, captain of the Babylonian guard, carried captive to Babylon the remainder of the people. He left only the poor of the land and gave to them the vineyards and fields to tend as vassals of Babylon. These events and other details are found in 39:1–10 and 52:1–34. The latter is a historical appendix added to the book and is an account of the fall of Jerusalem. This same material in 52:1–34 is found also in 2 Kings 24:18 to 25:30.

Jerusalem had fallen! For forty years Jeremiah had sought to warn his people with love and tears, but judgment had come. Idolatrous people had burned the Temple of Jehovah. A sinful people had carried into captivity the people of the living God.

What was to be the future of Jeremiah? Raymond Calkins says, "Death would have been an easy end compared to the lot which still awaited him." There remained one final chapter of his prophetic ministry. The remaining record concerning the life of Jeremiah is found in chapters 40–45. The material is chronological with the exception of 39:15–18, the promise to Ebed-melech, which was discussed above.

This period of the prophet's life reflects his "correspondence fixed with Heaven" in the day of his nation's greatest calamity. The city that was full of people sat solitary (Lam. 1:1). Jeremiah loved his city, and he loved the Temple. He rebuked the people for their form of worship, but he had a great love for the house of Jehovah. It was the perversion of respect for the Temple into a fetish superstition regarding it that called forth his fiery condemnation. He, like every good religious man of his day, faced a difficult adjustment when the Temple went up in flames.

When Nebuchadnezzar took Jerusalem, he gave command to his general, Nebuzaradan, to release Jeremiah. Jeremiah was committed unto Gedaliah, the Babylonian governor of Judah, and he lived with his own people. Jeremiah was later given the choice of going to Babylon and being well received and well treated or staying with the people who remained in Judah. The prophet's decision was to remain with his people. Subsequent chapters tell of the prophet's difficulties. Conspiracy seized the land. Gedaliah was murdered by Ishmael, who had been hired by the king of Ammon. Johanan then became the leader of the people. Chapter 42 tells how the people, because of their fear of the Babylonians, planned to go to Egypt. They went to Jeremiah for advice when in reality they wanted a confirmation of their own decision.

The prophet still had his "correspondence fixed with Heaven." True to his prophetic calling, he said, "I will keep nothing back from you" (42:4). He then told the people they had no need to fear the Babylonians and counseled them to remain in Judah. They ignored his advice and went in a body to Egypt. The last picture of Jeremiah which we have is of his brief ministry in Egypt, where he continued to warn the people of coming judgment because they had rejected God's will.

The secret of Jeremiah's spiritual stability was in his personal communion with God. One's prayer life both reflects and determines his religious outlook. God's will is never a static fact. It is always a growing experience. Jeremiah's "correspondence with Heaven" gave him inner strength, spiritual resources, and calm confidence in confusion, crisis, and calamity.

12

"New . . . in My Father's Kingdom"

There is nothing so powerful as an idea whose time has arrived. It required a lifetime for Jeremiah to understand fully and comprehend completely God's message, but patience always has her perfect work, and every generation stands eternally indebted to the prophet for the noblest concept of religion to be found in the Old Testament and the one which, more nearly than any other, anticipates the teaching of Jesus concerning the kingdom of God and the birth from above.

The new covenant of Jeremiah, strictly speaking, is located in 31:31–34, and yet in a broader sense the context includes all of chapters 30 and 31. These chapters are a part of the larger roll (chaps. 30–33) which is called by most scholars "The Book of Comfort." The two units, 30–31 and 32–33, were spoken at different times but were placed together in the compilation because all the material in the four chapters deals with the same theme—God's promise for the future restoration and blessing of his people.

The book of Jeremiah is more than the collection of a man's sermons or the account of a historical epoch in the life of a nation. It is the record of the religious development and spiritual quest of a great soul. This message concerning the new covenant was delivered by Jeremiah after the fall of Jerusalem and the destruction of the Temple. It represents the climax of his ministry and his deepest insight into the nature of God and his purposes for mankind. Between the first enthusiastic oracles of the young preacher boy (626 B.C.) and the deeply spiritual concept of a new covenant (586 B.C.) there was much deepening in the life of the prophet from Anathoth. The young preacher was impulsive, impatient, intolerant, and easily deceived by the superficial reforms of patriotic zeal which passed off as religious devotion. The prophet of the new covenant had lived through the reign of four kings and three invasions of his city.

Unless one understands the background of chapters 30 and 31, he misses much of the full force of the message. The words of Lord Macaulay are as relevant to Jeremiah and his ministry as to any man who ever lived:

It is difficult to conceive any situation more painful than that of a great man, condemned to watch the lingering agony of an exhausted country, to tend it during the alternate fits of stupefaction and raving which precede its dissolution, and to see the symptoms of vitality disappear one by one, till nothing is left but coldness, darkness, and corruption.[1]

Dr. Morehouse says that it was Jeremiah's lot to "stand in the way over which his nation was rushing headlong to destruction; to make an heroic effort to arrest it and to turn it back; and to fail, and be compelled to step to one side and see his own people whom he loved with the tenderness of a woman, plunge over the precipice into the wide, weltering ruin."

148

It was necessary for Jerusalem to be devastated and the Temple burned before Jeremiah could completely understand the true nature of spiritual religion. After the death of Josiah and the spiritual revolution which took place within the inner recesses of the prophet's soul, Jeremiah began to perceive these deeper truths. It was not, however, until the final chapter of Israel's doom that the revelation of God's message could be fully absorbed by this sensitive soul. Moulton pictures Jeremiah as he "stands amid the ruins of the shattered state . . . and declares that though the old national religion is past, yet behind it there is rising a grander and fuller religion, where every loyal heart shall delight to know and do God's will, and the golden age at last be realized." Pfeiffer agrees with this portrayal and states graphically:

Jeremiah seems to have discovered, in the moment when his world was crumbling about him, that it is always darkest just before dawn. In the ruin of his people, which he had visualized in advance as a nightmare of death, silence, darkness, and chaos, he recognized the birth pangs of a new and better order—a religion "in spirit and in truth" which he, more than any other man up to his time, had foreshadowed in agony of soul and in flashes of blissful illumination.[2]

Particular attention will be given to 31:27–40. These two chapters (30 and 31) were probably delivered after the fall of Jerusalem and before the journey to Egypt. They form one book, to which were added chapters 32 and 33 because of their similar subject matter. Perhaps the most fruitful study of all Jeremiah's prophecies would be a careful examination of these four chapters. In the larger sense chapters 30–31 contain the context of the new covenant. In the stricter sense the latter part of chapter 31 contains the actual covenant.

It is impossible to read 30:1 to 31:26 without immediately

sensing the historical situation. It was the time of Jacob's trouble (30:7). She was the bondman of strangers, and the yoke of the enemy was upon her neck (30:8). The prophet heard the voice of trembling and fear and not of peace. He saw every man with his hands on his loins like a woman in travail. He saw all faces turned into paleness (30:5–6). Judah's hurt was incurable, and her wound was grievous. There was none to plead her cause, that she might be bound up. She had no healing medicine. All her lovers had forsaken her. Jehovah had wounded her with the wound of an enemy, with the chastisement of a cruel one, for the greatness of her iniquity and because her sins were increased (30:12–15). The conclusion was inescapable concerning the background of these words. Jerusalem had fallen. The Temple was in ruins. Judah's hope had gone up in smoke even as Iarael was spoiled in the days of Assyria's might and power.

In the midst of Zion's loneliness the voice of Jehovah was heard: "Lo, the days come." He had a promise for Israel's future. "I will turn again the captivity of my people . . . I will cause them to return to the land that I gave to their fathers" (30:3); "I will break his yoke from off thy neck" (30:8); "I will save thee from afar, and thy seed from the land of their captivity" (30:10); "I am with thee, . . . for I will make a full end of all the nations whither I have scattered thee, but I will not make a full end of thee" (30:11); "I will restore health unto thee, and I will heal thee of thy wounds" (30:17). To Jeremiah, God was alive and active in the affairs of history. Although at present it was Zion whom no man sought after (30:17), yet Jehovah would have compassion on his dwelling places. The city would be built upon its own hill (its old site), and the palace would stand where it used to be (30:18). The people shall come and sing aloud on the height of Zion, and they shall be radiant over the goodness of the Lord (31:12). Jehovah will be the God of all the families of Israel (31:1). He had loved them with an everlasting love; therefore, he had remained faithful in that love in spite of their sin. "Is Ephraim my dear son? is he a darling child? for as often as I speak against him, I do earnestly remember him still: therefore my heart yearneth for him; I will surely have mercy upon him, saith Jehovah" (31:20).

Did ever a prophet of God speak with such tenderness and with such hope for the future? In the days of Judah's pride, Jeremiah shouted: "I have seen thine abominations. . . . Woe unto thee, O Jerusalem! . . . This evil people, that refuse to hear my words, that walk in the stubbornness of their heart, and are gone after other gods to serve them, and to worship them . . . Humble yourselves, sit down; for your headtires are come down, even the crown of your glory" (13:27, 10, 18). But in the day of her calamity Jeremiah reassured his people: "Refrain thy voice from weeping, and thine eyes from tears; . . . Again shalt thou plant vineyards upon the mountains of Samaria. . . . Yet again shall they use this speech in the land of Judah and in the cities thereof . . . Jehovah bless thee, O habitation of righteousness, O mountain of holiness" (31:16, 5, 23).

There are three main divisions in the new covenant (31: 27–39). Each of these sections (vv. 27–30; 31–37; 38–39) begins with the expression, "Behold, the days come, saith Jehovah."

Individual (31:27–30)

These verses are, of course, a prelude to the actual covenant, as verses 35–40 are a postlude, yet they contain an integral part of the message. According to verse 26, the prophet awoke "and beheld; and my sleep was sweet unto me." Some scholars believe that all of 30:1 to 31:25 was revealed to Jeremiah in a dream. There is strong evidence for this position, and this would mean that these three following sections contain both the sequel to what has gone before and the climax of the entire two chapters. The Lord was preparing to build and plant Judah again, but this time it would be on a different basis. Thus far in her religious history and outlook there had been little concept of individualism. The basic unit had been the family; at all cost the family name must be upheld and preserved. The Levirate marriage law was in order that "his name be not blotted out of Israel" (Deut. 25:6). When Achan was found guilty of stealing the Babylonish garment and the silver and gold (Josh. 7:16–26), it was not merely Achan but his family as well who was stoned. This sense of component guilt with little freedom of the individual had caused a proverb to spring up in Israel: "The fathers have eaten sour grapes, and the children's teeth are on edge" (Ezek. 18:2). A person excused judgment upon himself by saying he was suffering for the sin of his father. On the other hand, he could violate God's law and be comfortable in the assumption that the punishment would be transmitted to his son. But Jeremiah was the prophet of individualism. "In those days they shall say no more, The fathers have eaten sour grapes, and the children's teeth are set on edge. But every one shall die for his own iniquity: every man that eateth the sour grapes, his teeth shall be set on edge" (31:29–30).

One of Christianity's chief cornerstones is this doctrine of individualism. The new covenant, with its emphasis upon the individual, anticipates the major emphasis of our Saviour's ministry. It is the assurance that Jesus cares for us as individuals that gives comfort in time of sorrow. A minister tells in a story that Mrs. Humphrey Ward wrote a letter to a member of Parliament regarding a family in her district, asking that he give the matter his particular attention. She had every reason to believe that he would follow through with the request, for he had always manifested great interest in social welfare and had sponsored much legislation concerning social progress. She was startled when he replied: "I am so busy with plans for the race that I have no time for the individual." Mrs. Ward filed the letter away with this observation written across it: "Our Divine Lord, when last heard from, had not attained this sublime attitude." Dr. H. C. Phillips states this great truth graphically: " 'God so loved the world'—that is a magnificent concept. But just suppose that were all we knew about God, that he loved the world. 'Christ . . . loved the church.' . . . That is more meaningful because more personal. 'Christ . . . loved me, and gave himself up for me.' . . . That rings the bell!"

Truth does not bless the world until it becomes incarnate. Emerson reminds us that "the universal does not attract us until housed in an individual." Henry Van Dyke calls individualism "the salt of common life." Walt Whitman says, "Underneath all, individuals. I swear nothing is good to me now that ignores individuals." Robert Browning testifies to God's evaluation of the individual when he says:

> All that I could never be
> All that men ignored in me
> That was I worth to God
> Whose wheel the pitcher shaped.

Bonaro Overstreet set forth this same truth:

You say the little efforts that I make
will do no good: they never will prevail
to tip the hovering scale
where Justice hangs in balance.
     I don't think
I ever thought they would.
But I am prejudiced beyond debate
in favor of my right to choose which side
shall feel the stubborn ounces of my weight.[3]

This doctrine of individualism in Jeremiah's new covenant prepares the way for the major doctrines of the Christian faith. What are the distinctives of Christianity? Are they not all based on the worth of the individual? Personal salvation, believers' baptism, autonomy of the local church, separation of church and state, priesthood of believers—all of these are implicit in Jeremiah's doctrine that the individual is supreme. When Thomas Jefferson was in the process of drafting the Declaration of Independence, he visited a Baptist church in a rural section. It was Saturday afternoon and time for the monthly business meeting in the little country church. Jefferson watched the freedom with which the members spoke and observed the equality of each person. He then went back home and wrote, "We hold these truths to be self-evident, that all men are created equal, that they are endowed by their Creator with certain unalienable rights, that among these are Life, Liberty, and the pursuit of Happiness."

The supreme expression of the doctrine of individualism is found in our New Testament concept of Christ as "personal Saviour." Although this exact expression does not occur in the New Testament, it is constantly on our tongues today in evangelistic efforts and emphases. Christ died for all, but only those who receive him personally shall be saved. During the early part of the seventeenth century there arose in England two groups of Baptists—the General Baptists and the Particular Baptists. The former said the atonement of Christ was for everyone but that only those who believe in him receive the benefits of his death. Over against this the latter group maintained that Christ died for the elect only. In reality, both were saying the same thing. Christianity is a matter of an individual relationship with God in Jesus Christ. Jesus is not only the Saviour of the world; he is my personal Saviour if I have entered into an experience with him through personal repentance and personal faith. Martin Luther once said, "The heart of the Christian faith is in its personal pronouns." Jeremiah was declaring that God's purpose and plan is upon an individual basis. The matter of one's relationship to God is personal. God will never poach upon the sacred precinct of personality.

Inward (31:31–37)

Any person, idea, or movement should be cautiously evaluated as superlative, but in these verses is found the zenith of all prophetic teachings. Jeremiah's new covenant, more than any other spiritual concept even to this day, presents religion as an inner principle—in the words of Charles Jefferson, "an affair of the heart." Kyle Yates observes that Jeremiah, being familiar with the idea of religion based on a covenant, saw that because the people had failed to recognize the reality of the individual responsibility, the old covenant had broken down. Yates says, "There was no hope of renewing the old covenant. A new one must be substituted for it. That covenant must be *personal, inward, universal, spiritual and efficacious*."

Jeremiah, more than any other prophet, discovered and

developed the truth that it is the heart which must be properly related to God if life is to be vital and fruitful. The word "heart," or its plural, is used sixty-two times in the book which bears Jeremiah's name. Only the books of Psalms and Proverbs use this word more, and these books represent a composite authorship. It should be noted, however, that Jeremiah's word for heart (sixty of the sixty-two times the root is the same) means more than the seat of feelings and emotion. It refers to a person's mode of thinking and acting, to the seat of the will, purpose, determination. To the heart is ascribed understanding, intelligence, and wisdom.

From the outset of Jeremiah's ministry, and continuing throughout, the prophet sensed and stated that Judah's iniquity and guilt were rooted in an alienated heart. In spite of Israel's folly and the resulting punishment, Judah had not returned to God with her whole heart (3:10). Concerning the people of Judah and Israel, he spoke of "the stubbornness of their evil heart" (3:17), "a revolting and a rebellious heart" (5:23), and a heart "departeth from Jehovah" (17:5). He concluded, "The heart is deceitful above all things, and it is exceedingly corrupt" (17:9), and pictured the sin of Judah as "written with a pen of iron, and with the point of a diamond . . . graven upon the tablet of their heart" (17:1). Jeremiah interpreted Jehovah as a trier of the heart (11:20) and counseled Jerusalem to "wash thy heart from wickedness" (4:14) and "circumcise yourselves to Jehovah, and take away the foreskins of your heart" (4:4). In the letter to the captives in Babylon, who were taken during the first two invasions of the city, Jeremiah wrote, "Ye shall seek me, and find me, when ye shall search for me with all your heart" (29:13).

In light of his constant and continuous emphasis upon the

heart, it is most natural that Jeremiah's interpretation of the ultimate in transformed character would be a changed heart: "I will put my law in their inward parts, and in their heart will I write it" (31:33). In an earlier message to the captives Jeremiah had approached the new-convenant concept when he said, "I will give them a heart to know me, that I am Jehovah: and they shall be my people, and I will be their God; for they shall return unto me with their whole heart" (24:7).

Across six centuries two mighty spirits meet and touch, for the underlying principle of the Master's ministry was his teaching concerning the heart. His followers are to love the Lord with all their hearts (Mark 12:30); it is the pure in heart who are blessed (Matt. 5:8); and it is out of the abundance of the heart that the mouth speaks, because the good man out of the good treasure of his heart brings forth that which is good (Luke 6:45). In the conversation between Jesus and Nicodemus, perhaps the greatest interview of all ages, Jesus spoke, as Morgan says, "face to face, mind to mind, heart to heart."

There are two basic elements in the New Testament teaching concerning the kingdom of God. One is the atonement through which man has assurance that his sins are forgiven, or as Paul says, men are "justified by his blood" (Rom. 5:8). The other is regeneration, or the new birth, wherein man's heart is changed through the transforming power of the Holy Spirit, or again as Paul says, they become "a new creation" (2 Cor. 5:17). These concepts are implicit in the new covenant of Jeremiah and are united in the ministry of Jesus.

Early in his ministry as our Saviour spoke concerning the new birth, he was bringing to fruition the words of Jeremiah. When Jesus said, "Ye must be born again," he was saying that God's law must be written upon the heart of the individual in such a way that it becomes a principle of life operating within the human soul. Peake says of verse 33: "The 'new birth,' 'the new heart,' as the Gospel proclaims them are implied in this great saying." This new birth becomes the basis for the priesthood of believers as the prophet says, "I will be their God, and they shall be my people. And they shall teach no more every man his neighbor, and every man his brother, saying, Know Jehovah; for they shall all know me, from the least of them unto the greatest of them, saith Jehovah" (31: 33–34). These words should not be interpreted as teaching that in the future there shall be no need for religious instruction. This would be inconsistent with the entire missionary message of the Scriptures. The prophet was saying rather that there shall be in the new covenant that which did not exist in the old covenant—a direct access to God. In the old covenant, as man approached God the distinctive feature was awe, and human mediation was necessary. In the new covenant, the barrier is broken down, and there is an immediate approach to him through Jesus the High Priest.

On the last night of his earthly ministry our Saviour was with his disciples in the upper room. As he broke the bread and poured the fruit of the vine, he said, "This is my blood of the new covenant." The conclusion is inescapable. As Jesus prepared to go to the cross, and as he gave his disciples an ordinance by which to remember him as the Saviour from sin, he instinctively called to their minds and hearts the new covenant of Jeremiah. There Jehovah had said, "I will forgive their iniquity, and their sin will I remember no more" (31:34).

The kingdom of God, the reign of God in the human heart, thus has its roots deep in Old Testament teaching. This presence of God in the human heart provides the two basic needs for vital Christian living. Through the atonement of Christ the individual has complete assurance of forgiven sin. Through the work of the Holy Spirit the individual experiences a transformation of heart which affects every area of affection and attitude. These elements, both clearly anticipated in Jeremiah's new covenant and united in the ministry of Jesus, are essential for the development of full Christian character.

At a recent seminar on Judaism a rabbi was encouraging discussion of the lectures and an evaluation of Judaism. One member of the group said, "Rabbi, we share your enthusiasm concerning the moral and ethical standards of your faith. We recognize, however, the fact of human frailty. Does your faith possess anything comparable to the Christian doctrine of the new birth—a power that enables one to live by his standards and up to his ideals?" The rabbi paused a moment reflectively, dropped his eyes, and shook his head negatively. "No," he replied sadly. "Ours is a religion of ethics—nothing more."

Let no one minimize the ethical compulsion of the gospel and the prophets. But it requires a new birth for one to say, "In the One who pours power into me, I am strong unto all things" (Phil. 4:13). The Hebrew people were sincere and genuinely dedicated to their ideals, but they lacked the vitality of a personal encounter with God. Such an experience comes only when men see the "glory of God in the face of Jesus Christ" (2 Cor. 4:6). When the fulness of Jesus shines backward across the pages of the Old Testament, one who has met the Master can see in Jeremiah's new covenant God's plan, promise, and program for both the individual and society.

Instrumental (31:38–40)

A consideration of this final section calls for dealing with one of the most difficult passages in the Old Testament and one concerning which interpreters are most sharply divided. The particular problem to be faced in interpreting these verses is the relation of God to Israel and the position of Israel in God's program for the future.

After Jehovah had declared his intention to write his law within the hearts of his people and to remember their iniquity no more, he made a strong promise to Israel. If the sun and moon and stars cease before Jehovah, then "the seed of Israel also shall cease from being a nation before me for ever" (31:36). If heaven above can be measured and the foundation of the earth searched out beneath, then will Jehovah cast off all the seed of Israel for all that they have done (31:36–37). These words cannot be misunderstood. The prophet was saying that whatever happens, Israel shall maintain a unique relationship to Jehovah and shall perform a definite function in his purpose.

In order to reinforce his words, Jehovah gave a picture of the rebuilt city (31:38–40) which would be extended in boundary to include some places as "holy unto the Lord" which in Jeremiah's day were considered unclean. Peake says, "The regeneration of Jerusalem is to go so far that even the unclean districts on the south, the valley of Hinnom defiled with human sacrifice, are to be taken into the city and yet not to compromise its sanctity. Rather they will be redeemed from their uncleanness by the mighty holiness resident within it, so that the whole city will be holy to Yahweh."

This promise of Israel's indestructibility and the words concerning the rebuilt and extended city seem clear enough.

160

The interpretation, however, is not quite as simple. Two schools of thought differ radically both in their approach and their conclusions.

There is the school which calls for, and insists upon, a literal interpretation and maintains that there is yet to be a literal fulfilment. The return from Babylonian captivity did not satisfy the requirements of verses 38–40. The fulfilment, therefore, rests in the future, and most interpreters who hold this view believe not only in a literal restoration of the Jewish nation but also in an earthly reign of Christ with his throne at Jerusalem. In support of this position is the contention that God made a promise to Israel that has never been completely fulfilled. His promise of restoration has never been completely accomplished, and the fulness of the land has never been completely realized. It is the further contention of this school that the promises of God to Abraham were unconditional and have never been cancelled. There is, therefore, a period in the future, perhaps soon, when Israel shall once more occupy her land. This shall be accompanied by unprecedented material prosperity and unparalleled fertility of the land. One of the ablest advocates of this view is Wilbur Smith, who says,

For centuries the scattered and persecuted people of Israel have looked toward Palestine with hope and expectation and with a prayer that God would restore them to the land promised to the patriarchs for a perpetual possession. . . . The names of Palestine, the prophecies regarding Palestine, the disappointing history of the Jews in Palestine in ancient times and events in the newly created state of Israel bear a united, indisputable testimony to the fact that the greatest glory this land has ever seen will yet be unfolded. Jerusalem shall truly become a city of peace, and the people of God will dwell in unwalled villages, each man sitting in quietness and confidence under his own tree. This will be God's victory for that portion of the earth which He has called His own land.[4]

All scholars, however, do not agree with those who demand a literal fulfilment of these verses. There is involved in the question the entire problem of Israel's instrumentality in the purpose of God and the obligation of Jehovah to bless and use a people who have disobeyed the commandment of the one who called and blessed them. The instrumentality is clearly seen in Jehovah's call to Abraham and the promise which accompanied that call. "I will make of thee a great nation . . . I will bless thee . . . be thou a blessing: and I will bless them that bless thee, and him that curseth thee will I curse: and in thee shall all the families of the earth be blessed" (Gen. 12:2–3). Two elements are involved in these verses. First, God will bless Abraham and his descendants. Second, they are to be a blessing unto others, even unto all families of the earth. From the outset is thus seen the obligation upon the recipient of a divine blessing.

While Israel was encamped in the wilderness of Sinai before the mount, Jehovah made clear the conditional element in his relation to Israel. "If ye will obey my voice . . . then ye shall be mine own possession" (Ex. 19:5). This doctrine of moral responsibility was developed throughout the Old Testament as Jehovah declared his purpose concerning Israel. Early in Israel's history the conditional element was not emphasized as strongly, but as the years passed Jehovah uttered sharp warnings as to the fate of the nation if it failed as his instrument.

How are these facts related to the promise of Jehovah concerning the rebuilding of the city? Israel was God's agency for blessing the world. Through her, God purposed to bring salvation to all peoples. His Son, our Saviour, came through the Jewish race, but God's redemptive plan included the whole world. In the second servant poem the prophet said, "It is too light a thing that thou shouldest be my servant to raise up the tribes of Jacob, and to restore the preserved of Israel: I will also give thee for a light to the Gentiles, that thou mayest be my salvation unto the end of the earth" (Isa. 49:6).

God did not call Abraham and bless Israel merely that he could glorify a people. Neither did he choose Israel in order that he might boast about a chosen race unto himself. He called and blessed Israel in order to reach the world with a spiritual message through the medium of his instrument. The plain teaching of Isaiah is that God can use an instrument as long as he wishes and as long as that instrument is usable. This was true of Assyria and Babylon as they were instruments of God for punitive purposes. God likewise used Israel as long as Israel was usable. The time came, however, when the Jews as a nation failed to be usable in the purpose of Jehovah. Some Jews became Christians, but most did not. The New Testament clearly teaches that the true Israel is that group which has accepted Christ as Saviour and Lord. Paul insisted that "they are not all Israel, that are of Israel" (Rom. 9:6). He maintained further, "He is not a Jew who is one outwardly; neither is that circumcision which is outward in the flesh: but he is a Jew who is one inwardly; and circumcision is that of the heart" (Rom. 2:28–29). To the Galatians who, due to the influence of the Judaizers, were confused concerning the relationship of Judaism to Christianity, Paul wrote, "If ye are Christ's, then are ye Abraham's seed, heirs according to promise" (Gal. 3:29).

The new covenant is the instrument in the purpose of God. Those who are born into the family of God through the blood of the covenant become his witnesses, and through redeemed people his kingdom is to be extended in the hearts of people. It is not necessary for God to restore the Jewish nation in order to prove his sovereignty. He can do so if he desires, but if Israel ever wins favor with God, it will be because she has accepted Christ as Saviour. God is not dealing with the Jew as a nation but as individuals. The Jew is on the same level with the Gentile. When the veil of the Temple was rent in twain (Matt. 27:51), the middle wall of partition was broken down (Eph. 2:14), and from henceforth as many "as were baptized into Christ did put on Christ. There can be neither Jew nor Greek, . . . bond nor free, . . . male and female; . . . all are one man in Christ Jesus" (Gal. 3:27–28).

> In Christ there is no East or West,
> In Him no South or North;
> But one great fellowship of love
> Throughout the whole wide earth.
>
> JOHN OXENHAM

Does this mean that God has no further plan for the Jewish nation? There are those who believe there will be, in the future, a great turning to the Lord on the part of Israel. Paul wrote to the Romans, "Hardening in part hath befallen Israel, until the fulness of the Gentiles be come in; and so all Israel shall be saved: even as it is written, There shall come out of Zion the Deliverer; he shall turn away ungodliness from Jacob: and this is my covenant unto them, when I shall take away their sins" (11:25–27). Clifton Allen says, "Paul's words do mean, in the judgment of this writer, that there will be a mighty turning on the part of the Jews to the Lord. The stubborn unbelief of the chosen people will give place to faith. The persistent effort of the Jews to 'establish their own right-

164

eousness,' not according to God's way, will give place to penitent and trustful acceptance of the righteousness of faith."

On the other hand, Ray Summers and E. A. McDowell base their interpretation of "all Israel shall be saved" on the meaning of *houtōs*, translated "so" in most versions. These scholars insist that the correct rendering is "in this manner" and maintain that Paul was declaring that Jew and Gentile must be saved alike (in this manner) through the Deliverer that is come out of Zion, even Jesus our Saviour and Lord. They say that these words have no reference to a national restoration or even to a great revival among the Jewish people. Many who hold this view believe that the "great mystery" of which Paul speaks in Romans, Ephesians, and elsewhere is the truth that Christians are the true Israelites and are heirs of the promises made to Abraham and his seed.

There are devout Christians and dedicated scholars on both sides of this question. It seems that Christendom will never be unified in this area of interpretation. Is the rebuilding of the city to greater boundaries than ever before to be fulfilled literally? Some would contend that this must be done or else the Scriptures are false, and Jeremiah is discredited as a prophet of God. Others, however, maintain that a spiritual fulfilment is far more important than a literal one. Jeremiah's words find fulfilment in the preaching of the gospel to the uttermost part of the earth. As the parts of Jerusalem considered unclean are included in the restored city, even so the Gentiles, considered unclean by the Jews, are to have a part in God's kingdom of righteousness. While at Joppa, on the housetop of Simon the tanner, Peter was reminded that what God has cleansed is neither common nor unclean (Acts 10:14–15). Charles Wesley wrote:

His blood can make the foulest clean,
His blood availed for me.

If this interpretation be accepted, Jeremiah concluded his ministry with a great missionary message. He, like his contemporary Habakkuk, looked to a time when "the earth shall be filled with the knowledge of the glory of Jehovah, as the waters cover the sea" (Hab. 2:14).

Regardless of which interpretation is correct, one thing is certain. As Israel was God's instrument in Jeremiah's day, so spiritual Israel is God's instrument today. In yesteryear the law went forth from Zion, but in our day spiritual Zion is the agency for proclaiming the gospel. New Testament churches are God's instruments for preaching the message of our Saviour. Those who have been redeemed through the blood of the new covenant have a story to tell to the nations. That story will conquer evil, shatter the spear and sword, turn the darkness into dawning and the dawning to noonday bright. Regenerated humanity will "beat their swords into plowshares, and their spears into pruning-hooks; nation shall not lift up sword against nation, neither shall they learn war any more" (Isa. 2:4). As, one by one, men are made new creatures in Christ, we shall see his kingdom come in the hearts of people and his will done on earth as it is being done in heaven.

It is not enough merely to stand by and wait for Christ to bring the kingdom at his appearing. Truth, though crushed to earth, shall rise again; and righteousness, though long delayed, must reign. Every child of God must be a Christian optimist and do his part to "publish glad tidings, tidings of peace, tidings of Jesus, redemption and release." As we are faithful in preaching the message to the uttermost part of the earth, planting the Rose of Sharon in distant climes, we shall see that "in the desert rich flowers are springing." We shall then see the rich dews of grace open brighter scenes for world conquest, and as heavenly gales are blowing with peace upon their wings, soldiers of Christ, in truth arrayed, shall sing from hearts of love.

> Lead on, O King Eternal,
> Till sin's fierce war shall cease,
> And holiness shall whisper
> The sweet amen of peace;
> For not with swords' loud clashing,
> Or roll of stirring drums;
> With deeds of love and mercy
> The heav'nly kingdom comes.
>
> ERNEST W. SHURTLEFF

A Chronological Arrangement of the Book of Jeremiah

(Chapters 1–45)

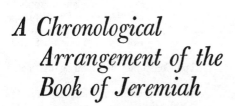

I. Prophecies During the Reign of Josiah

1:1–19	The Call of Jeremiah
2:1—4:4	The Call to National Repentance
4:5—6:30	The Foe from the North
11:1–8	The Proclamation of the Covenant
17:19–27	The Sabbath Day Discourse
11:18—12:6	The Plot against the Prophet
8:4–13	The Perils of Legalism
8:14—9:1	The National Collapse after Megiddo
22:10–12	The Lament for Jehoahaz

II. Prophecies During the Reign of Jehoiakim

22:1–9, 13–23	The Warning to Jehoiakim
7:1—8:3; 26:1–24	The Temple Sermon
18:1–23	The Parable of the Potter
19:1—20:18	The Sermon from the Broken Bottle
13:1–17	The Linen Girdle and the Shattered Jar
25:1–38	The Fate of Judah and the Nations
36:1–32; 45:1–5	The Dictation of the Roll and a Message to Baruch
35:1–19	The Fidelity of the Rechabites

14:1—15:9	The Message on the Drought
15:10–21	The Prayer of the Persecuted Prophet
16:1—17:8	The Inevitable Doom for Sinful Judah
17:9–18	The Prophet's Appeal for Deliverance
9:2–26; 10:17–25	The Wrath of Yahweh upon a Sinful People
11:9–17	The Conspiracy of Judah against Yahweh
12:7–17	The Devastation of Judah by Hostile Neighbors

III. Jehoiachin—and After

22:24–30	The Prophecy against Jehoiachin
13:18–27	The Dirge on the Approaching Doom
24:1–10	The Two Baskets of Figs
29:1–32	The Letter to the Exiles
27:1—28:17	The Necessity of Submission to Babylon
23:9–40	The Discourse against the False Prophets
23:1–8	The Prophecy Concerning Zedekiah
10:1–16	The Message against Idolatry
21:1–14	The Prediction of the Fall of Jerusalem
34:1–7	The Message to Zedekiah during the Siege
37:1–10	The Message to Zedekiah during the Temporary Lifting of the Siege
34:8–22	The Rebuke to Judah Concerning the Hebrew Servants
37:11–21	The Arrest of Jeremiah
38:1–28	The Prison Life of Jeremiah
39:15–18	The Promise to Ebed-melech
32:1—33:25	The Prophecies of Hope from the Court of the Guard

Notes

Introduction

1. All Scripture quotations are from the American Standard Version of the Bible unless otherwise noted.

2. Harry Emerson Fosdick, *The Modern Use of the Bible* (New York: The Macmillan Company, 1924), p. 21.

Chapter I

1. John Skinner, *Prophecy & Religion* (Cambridge: The University Press, 1941), p. 28.

2. Rudolf Kittle, *Great Men and Movements in Israel*, trans. Charlotte A. Knoch and C. D. Wright (New York: The Macmillan Company, 1929), p. 336.

Chapter IV

1. Skinner, *op. cit.*, pp. 89–90.

2. C. Von Orelli, *The Prophecies of Jeremiah*, trans. J. S. Banks (Edinburgh: T. & T. Clark, 1889), pp. 146–47.

3. W. O. Carver, *Sabbath Observance* (Nashville: Broadman Press, 1940). pp. 85–86.

4. See C. F. Kent, *The Kings and Prophets of Israel and Judah* (New York: Charles Scribner's Sons, 1909), p. 243.

5. Harry Emerson Fosdick, *A Faith for Tough Times* (New York: Harper & Brothers, 1952), pp. 111–12.

Chapter V

1. Hazen G. Werner, *Real Living Takes Time* (Nashville: Abingdon-Cokesbury Press, 1948), p. 138.

2. Elton Trueblood, *Foundations for Reconstruction* (New York: Harper & Brothers, 1946), p. 41.

3. *Ibid.*

Chapter VIII

1. Skinner, *op. cit.*, p. 249.

Chapter X

1. A. B. Davidson, *Old Testament Prophecy* (Edinburgh: T. & T. Clark, 1904), pp. 16–17.

2. A. W. Blackwood, *Preaching from Prophetic Books* (New York: Abingdon-Cokesbury Press, 1951), p. 21.

Chapter XII

1. A. W. Streane, *The Book of the Prophet Jeremiah Together with the Lamentations* (*Cambridge Bible for Schools and Colleges*, ed. A. F. Kirkpatrick [Cambridge: The University Press, 1926]), p. viii.

2. R. H. Pfeiffer, *Introduction to the Old Testament* (New York: Harper & Brothers, 1941), p. 517.

3. Bonaro Overstreet, "Stubborn Ounces" from *Hands Laid upon the Wind* (New York: W. W. Norton & Co., 1955); used by permission.

4. Wilbur Smith, "Israel in Her Promised Land," *Christianity Today*, I (Dec. 24, 1956), 10–11.